Editor
Cynthia Davidson

Managing Editor
Patrick Templeton

Editorial Interns
Riley Grills
Stanley Spence
Motuma Tulu

Protagonists
Thomas Daniell
Todd Gannon
Catherine Ingraham
Sanford Kwinter
Manuel Orazi
Bryony Roberts
Julie Rose
Sarah Whiting

www.anycorp.com

Summer this year has been a charged political season. Closely watched elections in the United Kingdom, France, Mexico, and Venezuela were just a few of the more than 80 national contests that have been or will be held in 2024, each with the potential to change not just national policies and international cooperation but also the future of our shared planet. And now we are in the throes of the United States' presidential race, with its stark policy differences between candidates Kamala Harris and Donald Trump.

    I have often said that more architects should engage in politics and more architects should run for public office, whether at the local, state, or national level, and not because so many lawmakers are called "architects" of legislation and policy. All architecture is political. As stewards of the built environment, architects, designers, landscape architects, and urban planners bear responsibility for how we live and how the present, and the past, shape our future. Our work is socioeconomic and environmental policy in built form.

    Architecture has been in a period of self-criticism. While it is always important to be introspective, to recalibrate how we think about and approach our work, on this threshold of change in the United States – and I hope it is *real* change – it is time for forward action. In a new book called *The Avant-Gardists*, author Sjeng Scheijen quotes early 20th-century Russian painter Mikhail Larionov as saying, "Life has invaded art. Now it is time for art to invade life." Today, in the early 21st century, it is time for *architecture* to "invade" life; to be the avant-garde that lobbies for and leads the changes in how we live together, build together, and care for our world, our shared Earth. – *CD*

Log 61 Copyright © 2024 Anyone Corporation. All Rights Reserved. ISSN: 1547-4690. ISBN: 978-1-7365007-9-8. Printed in USA. *Log* is published three times a year by Anyone Corporation, a nonprofit corporation in the State of New York with editorial and business offices at 1133 Broadway, Suite 330, New York, NY 10010. Subscription for 3 issues: $45 US; $49 CAN/MEX; $69 International. Single issues are available in print or as PDFs for $18, plus shipping if applicable. The opinions expressed herein are not necessarily those of the protagonists or of the board of the Anyone Corporation. Send inquiries, letters, and submissions to log@anycorp.com.

Log

Summer 2024 — Observations on architecture and the contemporary city

Author	Page	Title
Tim Altenhof	63	Out of the Ordinary: A Day with Peter Haimerl
Iman Ansari	27	Toward a Program of Action
Justin Beal	131	Architecture at the End of the World
Kristine Chung	47	On Bell Towers and Cell Towers
Thomas Daniell	37	Fantastic Voyage
Ben Fehrman-Lee	95	Vision in the Hands of the Visionary
Todd Gannon	115	Remembering José Oubrerie
Jimenez Lai	107	Swings, Stacks, and Spools at Coachella
Lina Malfona	101	All the Colors between Black and White
André Patrão	121	The Language of the End of Architecture
Christopher Pierce	51	Cabin Fever
Analia Saban	144	*This One (Edition of 100)*
Motuma Tulu	75	Eight Days on the Butajira
Andrew Witt	16	Dream Beams and Megadomes
Cameron Wu	6	Sphere of Influence

General Observations:
Matt Conway on Digital Drawing 94 . . .
Cynthia Davidson on Quick Books 114 . . .
D. Joseph Dignan on a View 106 . . .
Ludwig Engel on Logistics 130 . . .
Riley Grills on Desire Paths 26 . . . and on Homegrown 93 . . .
Win Overholser on Three Little Houses 74 . . .
Stanley Spence on a Tower 46 . . . and on Capsules 120 . . .
Patrick Templeton on a "Midnight Moment" 25 . . .

Cover Story:
Postcard: Kathleen Gilje, *Global Warming, after Albrecht Dürer's Portrait of Oswolt Krel*, 2013. Oil on panel, 17 by 13 1/2 inches. Courtesy the Herbert F. Johnson Museum of Art, Cornell University.

61

How do we understand the making of architecture today?

Image: Still from the documentary film *Into the Island*, 2023 © CCA

We've launched our new web issue, FORCES OF FRICTION to reflect on how contemporary voices from both within architecture and beyond confront the conditions that challenge and define the context of their work. We approach friction as both a catalyst and a method, bringing together architects and professionals from other disciplines in conversation to dwell upon the forces and conflicts that shape our built environments. In the opening article, "A Story of Encounters," Francesco Garutti expands on the question above, and introduces *Groundwork*, our latest exhibition and film series.

cca.qc.ca/friction

Architecture for Living

From Park Books

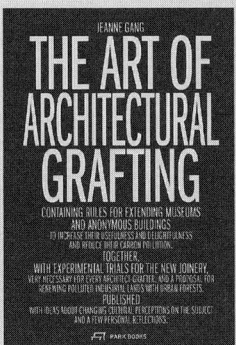

The Art of Architectural Grafting
Jeanne Gang

"Gang urges her peers to implement more impactful carbon-reducing strategies such as forgoing the demolition of buildings and increasing existing buildings' intensity of use. To demonstrate, she brings readers into her garden."—*Surface*

Cloth $40.00

ABC
Schools of the Future: Best Design Practices
Edited by Gaëtan Le Penhuel Architectes & Associés

Paris-based Gaëtan Le Penhuel Architectes & Associés have made their name with revolutionary designs of school buildings. Based on this wealth of experience, Gaëtan Le Penhuel presents this compact and charming guide to developing school buildings for the future that meet the needs of students.

Cloth $30.00

Distributed by the University of Chicago Press
www.press.uchicago.edu

From Paul Holberton Publishing

IRTH
Unveiling the Narratives of Architectural Materiality
Edited by the Curatorial Team of the National Pavilion of Saudi Arabia at la Biennale di Venezia

In a curatorial journey told through essays from visionary architects, researchers, and experimental material alchemists, the book represents the multiple viewpoints and projects emerging from Saudi Arabia and its wider region.

Cloth $55.00

From the National University of Singapore Press

The Airport as Urban Territory
The Spatial Effects of Singapore's Changi Airport
Anna Gasco

This book offers an analysis of Changi Airport's spatial influence at different scales and on different kinds of spaces, including rural areas, industrial and leisure zones, and the hinterlands of Singapore's shiny metropolis. It uncovers the airport's many actors, the complex networks of terrestrial linkages and interactions centered around the global hub, and the governance frameworks used to manage it.

Cloth $68.00

Populous, Sphere at The Venetian, Las Vegas Strip, 2023. Measuring 366 feet tall, it is the largest spherical structure in the world. Photo: Iwan Baan.

Cameron Wu

Sphere of Influence

For all its geometric simplicity, the sphere is largely incompatible with many fundamental requirements of architecture. The sphere, defined as all points equidistant from a single center, is arguably the simplest and purest geometric primitive. With no discrete sides, however, a sphere is not considered one of the traditional Platonic solids, which are defined as convex regular polyhedra with congruent regular polygons as planar faces. This exclusion by Plato may seem like an oversight, as a more contemporary geometric sensibility might reasonably consider a sphere as a polyhedron with infinite sides that are infinitesimally small – as small as a point. A sphere thus manifests the upper limit condition for the number of sides of a regular polyhedron, just as a tetrahedron manifests the lower limit, with the fewest sides numbering four. In Plato's defense, ancient Greek mathematicians worked mostly through the discipline of solid geometry, and having disallowed notions of variability and arithmetic continuity (the use of non-whole or irrational numbers), it was nearly impossible to develop a mathematics capable of addressing such granularity. Although certain techniques of solid geometry used for area and volume calculation (such as Eudoxus's "method of exhaustion") would conceptually resemble future related innovations, two millennia would pass before Gottfried Wilhelm Leibniz and Isaac Newton codified the mathematics of the infinitesimal by developing the calculus in the 1600s.

With no intrinsic orientation, the sphere's relationship to the ground is arbitrary. A complete sphere touches a horizontal (ground) plane tangently at a single point. Once this relationship with verticality is established, other architectural elements such as horizontal floors and interior vertical walls (normal and parallel with the vertical axis, respectively) may reinforce this orientation. Apertures penetrating the exterior surface may further define cardinal axes in plan. Yet nearly all features that orient and architecturally differentiate the sphere are imported from elsewhere, extrinsic to its geometric nature and subdivision.

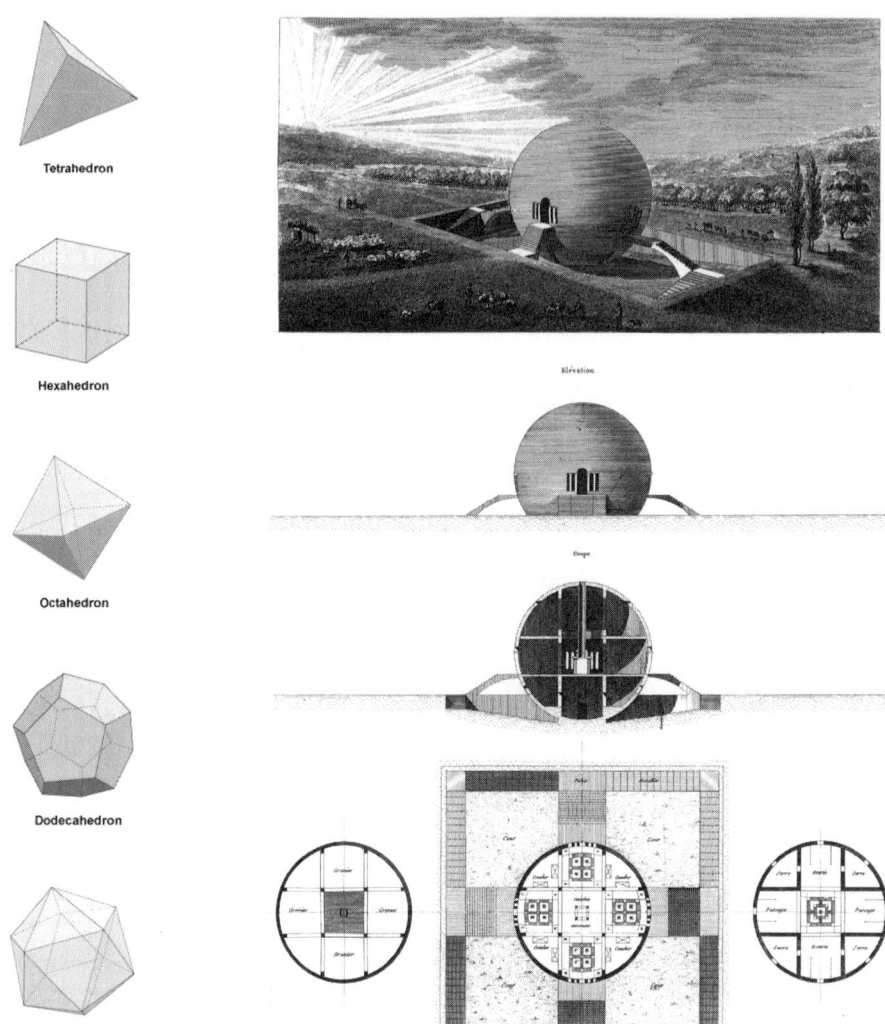

The five platonic solids are convex regular polyhedra with congruent regular polygons as planar faces. Right: Claude-Nicolas Ledoux, Maison des Gardes Agricoles, 1804. All images courtesy the author unless otherwise noted.

Some factors related to sphere subdivision logics are less arbitrary. The locations of Earth's geographic poles are defined by the planet's axis of rotation. A radial array of planes containing this axis "cuts" the sphere to produce the great circles of the lines of longitude, each intersecting both poles. Another series of cutting planes, perpendicular to the axis of rotation, defines circular lines of latitude running east-west, including the great circle of the equator, with successively smaller circles moving toward each pole. Although this axis is intrinsic to the Earth as a kinetic body, the cutting plane is just one of the infinite ways to subdivide its surface.

The sphere's antagonistic relationship with architectural requirements extends beyond pure geometric abstraction to

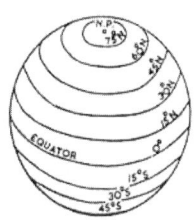
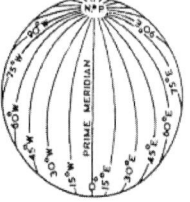

Lines of longitude and of latitude.

more pragmatic issues. Perhaps as conceptual extensions of apparent geometric purity and perfection, spherical domes and circular arches often represent the epitome of structure, though they do not perform particularly well. Spherical domes and circular arches induce eccentric bending in and tensile stresses on masonry stones and mortar, which prefer pure compression when carrying loads laterally and vertically to the ground. These structural inefficiencies have historically been overcome through sheer building mass, whereby thick and heavy stone voussoirs keep the suboptimal forms in adequate compression. When the Gothic style superseded the Romanesque in the Middle Ages, pointed arches served as prototype approximations of parabolic arches, catenary curves, and other funicular forms to come, allowing a reduction of building mass and a lightening of structural expression. Numerous examples of spherical geometries used in modern structures required surfaces and edges to be inelegantly thickened and reinforced to compensate for the lack of structural performance – the Sydney Opera House, MIT's Kresge Auditorium, etc. Despite the geometric and structural liabilities, a succession of speculative and constructed spherical architecture has persisted since antiquity. From the Pantheon to Étienne-Louis Boullée, from Buckminster Fuller to Disney's EPCOT Center, spheres have been deployed as pure and recognizable architectural icons.

The most recent and notable addition to this canon of orbs is Sphere at The Venetian just off the Las Vegas Strip. Designed by Populous for Madison Square Garden Entertainment Corp., it is a state-of-the-art entertainment venue and advertising apparatus, and, measuring 516 feet in diameter, it is the largest spherical building in the world. The exterior surface, known as the Exosphere, is truncated by the ground plane, resulting in a maximum height of only 366 feet, making it appear as if the lower third of its volume is lodged firmly in the earth. It has become an unmistakable new icon of Las Vegas.

Similar to other urban domes, the Sphere has two surfaces – one convex exterior and one concave interior. Both are equipped with LEDs capable of producing bright graphic displays that operate at different scales. The significant architectural/visual experiences occur in opposing locations and at scales that correspond to these surfaces: the one from without presenting the Sphere as a recognizable urban icon from afar, and the one from within offering a deeply immersive interior experience for the stationary subject. One is objective,

Top, left to right: Pantheon section with inscribed sphere; Étienne-Louis Boullée, Cenotaph for Sir Isaac Newton, Paris, France, 1784. Image courtesy Bibliothèque Nationale de France. Below, left to right: Buckminster Fuller, Montreal Biosphere, Montreal, Quebec, 1967; Wallace Floyd Design Group, Spaceship Earth, EPCOT, Walt Disney World, Florida, 1982.

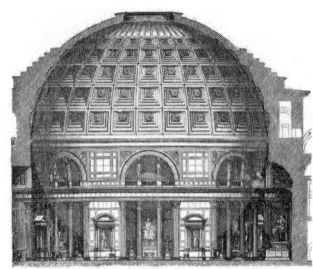

the other subjective. Of course, this duality of exterior urban objectivity and interior subjectivity is nothing new for domes. Filippo Brunelleschi's dome still serves as the primary figural beacon of Florence, providing urban orientation from multiple points in the city while also defining the spatial identity of its proximate public piazzas. Alternatively, the interior of the dome presents a highly articulated narrative fresco depicting the Last Judgment. The Sphere continues this trend of domical duality yet takes the schism to the extreme.

In terms of urban planning and design, the Sphere is unremarkable. As with most buildings on the Las Vegas Strip, there are two main approaches – one pedestrian and one vehicular – both prioritizing the interior isolation of patrons from the desert heat for as long as possible. Little consideration is given to spatial or aesthetic experience during either approach. A lengthy interior sequence leads from the casino floor at the Venetian Resort, past generic meetings rooms and event halls, to an enclosed pedestrian bridge that connects to the Sphere's entry concourse. The windows along this route offer scant and fleeting views of the Sphere's exterior, essentially providing a completely interior experience. Not surprisingly, any exterior pedestrian approach is inconvenient at best and, in the 100-plus degree desert temperatures, downright hostile at worst.

At the expansive vehicular drop-off and parking lot, one is confronted with the massiveness of the orb and can perceive the technology that enables the light displays. The structure of the Exosphere is a triangulated steel grid with 1.2 million LED pucks distributed evenly over the spherical geometry. This structural frame and the array of lights exist

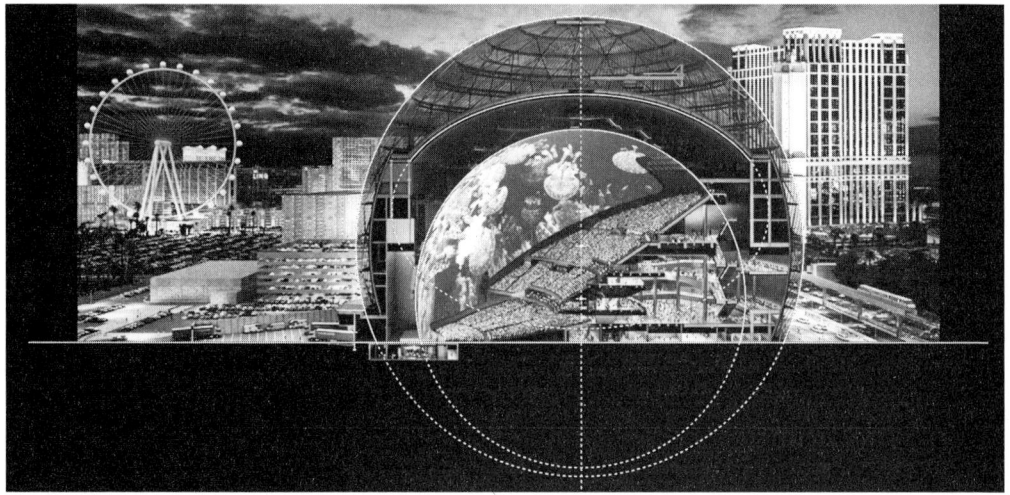

Section diagram showing the Sphere's nested geometries. A third intermediate between the two primary spheres is mostly imperceptible and serves as the weather barrier. This roof appears to be ellipsoidal, perhaps reinforcing the Sphere's structural liabilities.

outside the weather barrier, making the exterior tectonic appear layered and porous during the daytime. This porosity also enables the most effective image display, especially at night, as there is no continuous surface to reflect interfering light. Up close, the eight-inch separation between LED pucks allows each discrete light to be perceived, which causes the image to pixelate if not totally dissolve into oblique indiscernibility. While it is powerful to confront such a constructed piece of abstract geometry, the Sphere is not digitally calibrated to maximize this proximate experience.

From just a few blocks away, however, the metrics of the Exosphere's LED density and the limits of human optical perception yield very different results. As related to the initial discussion of multisided Platonic polyhedra, it turns out that 1.2 million points of light constitute an adequate approximation of the infinite. At an increased distance, the 256 possible colors of each discrete puck blend seamlessly to produce rich, saturated, and continuous images across the surface of the Sphere. Most of us have seen these images by now – surreal and uncanny juxtapositions of luminous objects in the desert enabled by digital tech and copious electricity.

Yet the exterior content displayed has not enabled the Sphere to transcend its urban objectivity or "object-ness" as a geometric primitive. The constant convex curvature and divergent exterior surface normals generally prohibit any significant optical effects from being widely perceived from the surrounding environs. Such modest perspectival effects might include a portion of the Sphere's curved surface appearing like a flat plane, or perhaps even concave. If the Sphere's surface is understood to be a canvas to be painted

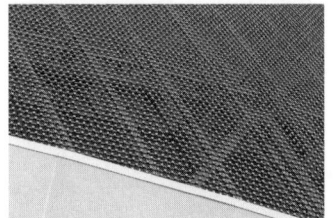

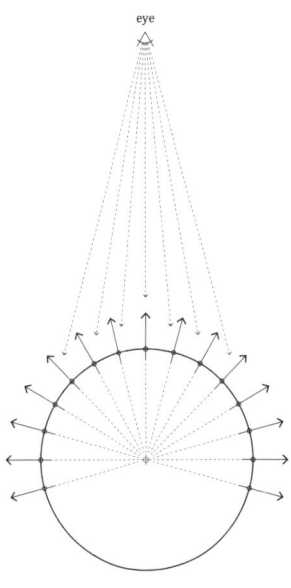

Diagram of a convex exterior surface, which has divergent normals that preclude visual coherence. Top, left to right: Sphere entry plaza; detail of the Exosphere armature; the diaphanous Exosphere; and a detail of the armature with LED pucks.

on, its convexity makes the outer limits of the image bend away from the viewing subject, essentially eradicating any perspectival coherence of any pictorial content. Unlike looking at a painting, when we look at the Sphere's exterior, we view most of its surface obliquely, especially the outer edges, rather than perpendicularly. Any privileged station points for which perspectival transformations might be calibrated would necessarily be highly localized and scattered about the city. Because the Sphere sits behind the expansive Venetian Resort, there is not even a primary urban axis or vista for the Sphere to respond to. Occasionally, when the display color is extremely homogenous and bright, the Sphere can appear to flatten into a two-dimensional graphic, as is the case when gigantic yellow emoji are displayed.

In short, from the outside, the Sphere generally looks like a sphere. The upshot is that the exterior imagery is often used to represent either scalar transformations of objects that are already spherical – eyeballs, basketballs, emoji, the Moon, the Earth, other planets – or two-dimensional images or patterns mapped spherically onto the surface. Again, the ambition of any perspectival or paradigmatic spatial transformation with LEDs is problematized by the convexity of the display surface, leading to the use of graphics and patterns that are abstract, scaleless, and without straight lines that would be subject to rules of perspective – content whose coherence is not put into visual crisis by being mapped onto a sphere. Any pictorial content is often made small and displayed on only one "side" of the Sphere, or in four locations 90 degrees apart in plan, essentially turning the Sphere into a four-sided billboard. (Think here, again, of architecture's tendency to impose cardinal orthogonality onto the

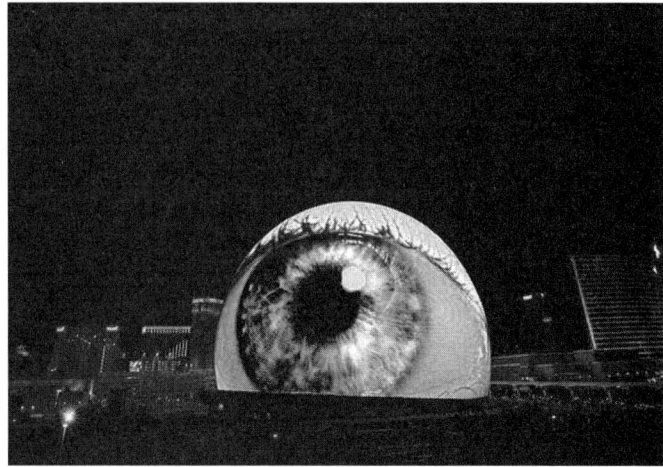
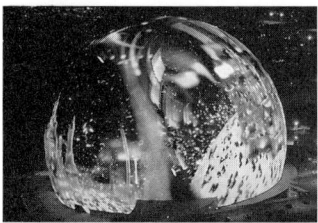

The Exosphere displays spherical objects and scaleless two-dimensional patterns with varied visual results. Photos: Sphere Entertainment.

indifferent geometry of the sphere.) Of course, sophisticated visual content that more radically transforms perceptions of the Exosphere could be authored and displayed to counter this criticism, but none has yet been seen. If used only to represent objects that are already spherical or as a three-dimensional billboard, it is unlikely that the Sphere can ever transcend its geometry. Unrealized potential of perspective and spatial transformations notwithstanding, the presence of giant and pristine spherical objects lodged in the city ground can be sublime and uncanny.

In terms of conventional interior architectural design, the Sphere is equally unremarkable. The entrance lobby and concourse atrium feel like an aestheticized shopless shopping mall, complete with cool-temperature mood lighting and long escalators. The interior LED screen has approximately 256 million pixels – orders of magnitude greater than the exterior – and is capable of providing pristine imagery with details and saturation. The concavity of this inner surface dictates that all surface normals converge on a single point in space, where, from a privileged position, one can view the entire display surface perpendicularly, and for which all perspectival effects are calibrated. The front row of the center 300-level seating section seems to be closest to this central point of convergence. Of course, there is only one true center, but the room's concavity allows most lines of sight from most seats to be near perpendicular to the display surface, resulting in only slight distortions of intended perspectival and spatial effects.

Numerous planetariums and IMAX theaters, at smaller scales, have long provided a similar type of immersive experience. Previously, these spherical surfaces functioned as passive

Interior graphics show concrete panels reminiscent of the Pantheon or zoom out from the Haight-Ashbury neighborhood of San Francisco (center) to an overview of San Francisco.

screens, receiving and reflecting projected light and requiring the negotiation of additional geometric, technological, and material difficulties associated with correctly projecting spherical content. The directness and immediacy of the LED screen bypass these burdens of projection and enable unprecedented scale and precision in the delivery of the visual content.

With its paradoxical specificity and neutrality of form, the Sphere's interior is the ultimate subjective architecture – or at least an architectural and technological apparatus that offers radically different subjective experiences. It is an architectural shape-shifter, capable of altering not only its perceived materiality but also its form and scale. When the effects are good, it could be described as architectural and neurological alchemy. The Sphere's interior can *convincingly* look as solid as the Pantheon or as delicate as scaffolding. Equally if not more exciting for architects, it can change its perceived shape and size. This is perhaps most poignant when the spherical room appears to transform into its paradigmatic opposite – a cube (or another rectangular/orthogonal geometry). The human brain is no match for the coherence and scale of the visual content displayed. It must submit to and process the information transmitted from the optical nerves, even if this information is spatially deceptive or misleading. It thus becomes impossible to understand the true geometry and spatial limits of the room.

Many of the effects shown during the events and concerts at the Sphere have conveyed the viewer to fantastical locations in Technicolor outer space or deep on the ocean floor. As an architect, however, I found the most powerful and convincing moments to be when the aforementioned simple geometric transformations, as well as those that represent quotidian spaces, were taken out of scale or context. The journey from townhouses in the Haight-Ashbury neighborhood up into the clouds allows one to understand the scales of San Francisco urbanism (like the Eames's *Powers of Ten*, but much more sensorial and less cognitive). One of the most powerful effects was being perceptibly transported to a room *much smaller* than the Sphere itself (Barton Hall, at Cornell University, site of a storied 1977 Grateful Dead concert). While the human brain cannot necessarily verify the size and scale of outer space, it can definitely sense when the room gets smaller.

In short, the Sphere's interior appears capable of presenting itself as nearly anything, architecturally and urbanistically speaking. Its spatial potentials are just beginning to be

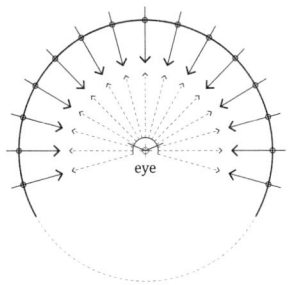

Diagram of the concave interior surface, which has convergent normals that enable visual coherence. Top: Interior graphic turns the concave surface into the orthogonal Barton Hall at Cornell University. Photo: Carter H.

catalogued. Because it is the newest architectural icon of Las Vegas, it seems appropriate to conclude this assessment of the Sphere in terms of Venturi, Scott Brown, and Izenour's well-known concepts of the duck and the decorated shed. From the exterior, the Sphere is definitely a duck. As a geometric primitive, it is not specifically figured or differentiated, yet its form is both recognizable and charged, especially in the context of architectural history and practice. Unable to transcend its "object-ness" as a sphere, coupled with its ability to display infinite variations of imagery and advertising, one might call the Sphere's exterior a decorated duck. On the interior, however, even though the geometric form is similar, its concavity makes it anything but a duck. If a shed is understood to be a neutral and flexible interior, the spatial shape-shifting capacities make the Sphere's interior the ultimate shed – finely and technologically decorated.

Cameron Wu is an assistant professor at the Princeton University School of Architecture and the author of the book *Lines of Development: Analysis, Geometry, Architecture*.

A massive glass sphere perched on the north end of Central Park houses the headquarters of a mysterious diversified corporation, from which a generation-long interplanetary tour of the cosmos would be planned. Doug Michels and Thomas Shannon, "The Humans: Precis" (unpublished manuscript, June 10, 1980).

Andrew Witt

Dream Beams And Megadomes

A hush falls over the theater. As the opening credits fade, the camera zooms in to a "high-velocity approach over the Atlantic," weaving through the towers of Manhattan and hurtling over Central Park toward a massive "1,000 foot diameter glass sphere" at the park's north end.[1] Just behind the glass skin of this cavernous structure sits a menagerie of "species from all over the world," arrayed in precious vitrines. As the camera lands in the "equatorial airport" of the massive sphere, the audience enters the world headquarters of a "superplanetary communications company,"[2] a diversified multinational with investments in "communications, energy, space ventures, fine arts, and pure research."[3] The dome is not only a corporate headquarters but also a communication nexus for "real but invisible forces . . . fields, micro, human, and macro, conveying emotional and metaphysical information . . . a connection, communications link up with the atomic civilization pervading the universe."[4] From this headquarters, the enigmatic company launches ventures ranging from interplanetary tours to "the education of a bioengineered living computer."[5]

So unfurls the vision of American architect and agent provocateur Doug Michels and his erstwhile collaborator Thomas Shannon in their draft script for "The Humans" (1980), a screenplay that imagines a multigenerational tour of the stars that returns to Earth to find it in ruins. Space stations, truth rays, brain probes, and flight shoes all appear as props in its improbable scenes. Michels, cofounder of the influential American art and architecture collective Ant Farm, had a gift for cinematic set pieces and hyperbolic imagination. An avatar of what his *New York Times* obituary termed, in 2003, the "lunatic fringe of art and architecture," Michels reveled in daring and absurd proposals that felt like both visionary futures and inside jokes.[6] Both during and after Ant Farm, Michels explored the overlap between video-electronic media and spatial fictions, often with a proto-posthuman sensibility that was deeply invested in interconnected sociotechnical ecologies. He playfully channeled an intuition for outsider science, a sharp wit, and

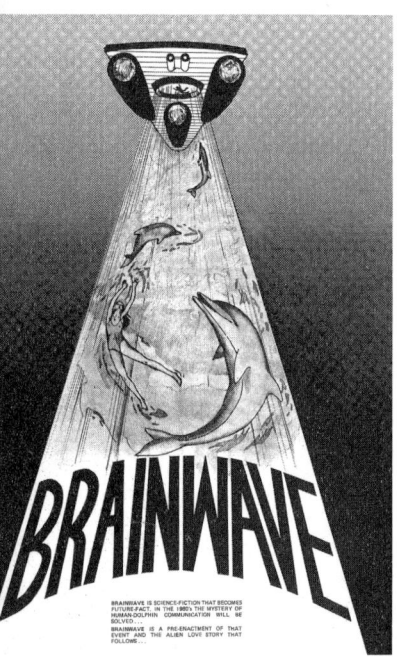

A promotional image for *Brainwave*, a film exploring the mental and social entanglements between dolphins and humans. Tony Morphett, Alexandra Morphett, and Doug Michels, *Brainwave* (Brainwave Productions, 1977), vi.

1. Thomas Shannon, "Chronicle of The Humans" (unpublished manuscript, June 9, 1980), 2.
2. Doug Michels and Thomas Shannon, "Humans Precis" (unpublished manuscript), 1.
3. Shannon, "Chronicle of The Humans," 2.
4. Ibid., 4.
5. Doug Michels and Thomas Shannon, "The Humans: Synopsis" (unpublished manuscript, June 17, 1980), 2.
6. Ken Johnson, "Doug Michels, Radical Artist and Architect Dies at 59," *New York Times*, June 21, 2003.
7. These manuscripts are in the Doug Michels Architectural Papers in the University of Houston archives.
8. Randolph Kinsuke Nakamura, "Architecture, Media, and Technologies of the Mind, 1948 – 1978" (PhD diss., University of California Los Angeles, 2020), 155. Kirsten Fleur Olds, "Networked Collectivities: North American Artists' Groups, 1968–1978" (PhD diss., University of Michigan, 2009), 163.

the instinct of a committed cultural gadfly. Across these projects, video and film were consistent protagonists and keys to decoding the architectural work itself.

Over a career of nearly 40 years, Michels developed a design practice convolving media and architecture with equal parts future-forward ambition and piquant irony. He worked within a capacious definition of architecture that sprawled beyond buildings to include videos, happenings, art installations, and news conferences. One of the most unusual yet little-documented aspects of Michels's multimedia work was a series of screenplays that included interplanetary tourism and interspecies ecologies. These screenplays, which he developed as unpublished manuscripts both during and after his involvement with Ant Farm, channeled aspects of the late 1970s mass media sci-fi milieu while revisiting many of the idiosyncratic preoccupations of Ant Farm, including speculative mobility, experimental communication, and fictional institutions.[7] The film treatments were serious attempts to shape the collective imagination toward alternative possibilities of the future through what historians Randy Nakamura and Kirsten Fleur Olds identify as "détournement or self-reflexive appropriation of mass media."[8] At the same time, these film projects were full of paradoxes. In them, Michels and his collaborators seemed to sincerely chase commercial aspirations while unabashedly embracing outré and idiosyncratic countercultural curiosities. Two film scripts, *Brainwave* and *Bluestar*, deal with themes of interspecies communication and computation, and suggest the strange possible tomorrows when technology, biology, and ecology might convolve in unexpected ways.

The screenplays of Michels and his collaborators propose visions of extraordinary architectures: extraterrestrial living environments, domical megastructures, labs and lagoons inhabited not only by humans but also by chatty animals and hyperintelligent machines. One of Ant Farm's best-known projects, the Dolphin Embassy, became a recurring and mutating setting for these screenplays. In its original incarnation, the Dolphin Embassy was a proposal for a floating research laboratory that created a common living and learning environment for dolphins and humans. Influenced in part by a broader cultural interest in communication with whales and dolphins during the 1960s and '70s, Ant Farm was particularly taken with the experimental work of John C. Lilly, a physician whose unorthodox techniques and technological experiments inspired hope that human-dolphin communication might be possible. Though it underwent perpetual revisions over the years, the Dolphin Embassy was a leitmotif to which Ant Farm and Michels anchored a constellation of media events, narratives, and representations.

At times, the Dolphin Embassy proposal leapt beyond fantasy into quasireality as a news event. Nakamura notes that, in the late '70s, the embassy developed as a "non-profit expedition funded by grants from the Rockefeller Foundation and the National Endowment for the Arts," which earned it a measure of public credibility.[9] Perplexed interviewers and bemused reporters wrestled with the unreality of it all, never quite sure if they were talking to visionaries, con men, or something altogether different. Far from incidental, news and media appearances were an essential corollary, if not an overt aim, of the Dolphin Embassy project. In a particularly comical press conference, Michels and Doug Hurr announced the launch of the embassy, seated in a faux TV production studio with a matrix of televisions arrayed behind them.[10] In the grainy video documenting this happening, a reporter gamely questions them about the details of the embassy as Michels and Hurr unpack the details with a deadpan delivery that amplifies the ludicrous nature of the proposal. Despite its implausibility, the Dolphin Embassy was convincing enough that the State of California briefly sponsored it as a research project. The then governor, Jerry Brown, accompanied by a phalanx of reporters, made an appearance to test an alleged prototype machine for interspecies translation. When one reporter said, "I heard that the Governor was going to talk to whales today," Ant Farmer Chip Lord responded flatly, "No, the whales are going to talk to him."[11]

Michels spent many years drumming up support for variants of the Dolphin Embassy in Australia, where media coverage continued apace. Michels and his Ant Farm colleagues made a series of memorable appearances on Australian television to promote the Dolphin Embassy and affiliated projects. One obviously nonplussed host introduced Ant Farm by announcing, with bewildered consternation, "Who they are is difficult to assess; why, is even harder."[12]

This constellation of media happenings surrounding the Dolphin Embassy recalls what historian Daniel Boorstin identified, in 1962, as "pseudo-events": events that are planned and staged exclusively for the purpose of being reported, reproduced, and propagated through visual media.[13] For Boorstin, these semistaged events contributed to an unreality that grew out of a collective and insatiable desire to "expect

9. Randolph Kinsuke Nakamura, "Architecture, Media, and Technologies of the Mind, 1948–1978" (PhD diss., University of California Los Angeles, 2020), 152.
10. "Video Communication Unit," Media Burn Archive.
11. "Jerry Brown talks to whales," directed by Optic Nerve (Internet Archive, Pacific Film Archive Film and Video Collection, 1977), videotape.
12. "A video letter from Doug Michels to Tom Weinberg," Media Burn Archive.
13. Daniel Boorstin, *The Image: A Guide to Pseudo-Events in America* (New York: Harper, 1961), 11.

14. Ibid., 4.
15. Tony Morphett, Alexandra Morphett, and Doug Michels, *Brainwave* (Brainwave Productions, 1977), iii.
16. Ibid., 99.
17. Ibid., 26.
18. Ibid., cover.
19. Ibid., iii.
20. "Project Bluestar," *Futurist* 21 (1987): 29.
21. Ibid.
22. Ibid., 31.
23. Ibid.

the contradictory and impossible."[14] Michels played on the expectations of a fantastic world as he gleefully punctured the boundary between reality and fiction. In a way, his media events became loosely planned and energetically improvised screenplays in their own right, with much the same effect of parafictional world-building.

Perhaps due to this enthusiastic media attention, Michels recognized the star qualities of the Dolphin Embassy and freely borrowed concepts from it in his own projects independent of Ant Farm. For instance, the Dolphin Embassy held center stage in Michels and collaborators Tony and Alexandra Morphett's 1977 screenplay *Brainwave*, in which the sociality of interspecies architecture is fleshed out considerably. The first line of the plot synopsis could have been written by Lilly himself: "Humans do not have to travel outward into space to meet an alien intelligence. There is already one here on Earth: the Dolphin."[15] Though never filmed, the screenplay is a window into the kind of architecture-adjacent provocation that Michels reveled in. The tagline describes how the "mystery of human-dolphin communication" would be solved as well as "the alien love story that follows."[16] Interspecies communication occurred through the technology of psychic television – dolphins could queue up video clips explaining their mental states – and through direct telepathy with certain crew members.[17]

Brainwave presented the embassy as a communications laboratory and an interspecies domestic space, a collective ecological living room. The embassy was a "half-way environment" between humans and dolphins. In it, we see a human nuclear family living their ordinary lives, albeit in an extraordinary setting. The "moonpools" for dolphin interaction recall the conversation pits that were all the rage in 1970s homes. Humans and cetaceans frolic together and eventually establish telepathic links, a prelude to the intimacies that follow.[18] The family's teenage daughter, Jane, seems to have a particularly strong cross-species psychic connection. "Jane and the Dolphin are maintaining their love for each other, despite the cultural collision involved. She comes from a species which shapes its environment, he from one which integrates with its environment. . . . Jane and the Dolphin run away together and live out a brief idyll in the waters surrounding a tropical island."[19]

Though the *Brainwave* vision of the Dolphin Embassy was already gleefully cavalier with any underlying science, that did not stop Michels from venturing even further off the

A drawing of the Dolphin Embassy, as it was to appear in the movie *Brainwave*. Strangely, the embassy is accompanied not only by a pod of dolphins but also by a sizable dragon. Tony Morphett, Alexandra Morphett, and Doug Michels, *Brainwave* (Brainwave Productions, 1977).

deep end with Project Bluestar, essentially a version of the Dolphin Embassy launched into orbit. An interspecies space station enclosed in a sphere of water, Project Bluestar was designed for the cohabitation of human, cetacean, and artificial intelligences, facilitated by interspecies communication systems. According to a 1987 article in *The Futurist*, the aim of this specific "space architecture" was explicitly cognitive: It was "designed to examine thought in zero gravity."[20] Michels claimed that, "programmed by the dolphin's ultrasonic sound waves, computers will generate holograms of thoughts and images for study by scientists aboard the spacecraft and on Earth."[21]

Playfully termed a "think tank in space," Project Bluestar was also a swim tank, or even a float tank akin to Lilly's sensory deprivation chambers. At the center of the station was the iconosphere, a 250-foot-diameter sphere of water that was weightlessly suspended and "ultrasonically stabilized."[22] It was home to a "crew of dolphins whose ultrasonic emissions will program a central computer, permitting the study of interface languages between biological and electronic systems. The exchange will find expression in computer-generated holographic images that use the aqueous sphere as a medium of projection – a lens – and as a medium of intelligence, communicating the fruits of *Bluestar*'s interactions."[23] Forgoing the mundanities of typical computer equipment, the water itself was a "substitute for a computer screen."[24]

With writing partner Joseph Cortina, Michels also compiled the over-the-top Hollywood-style screenplay *Bluestar*, for which he sought funding for years. According to a pithy plot synopsis: "Bluestar is a gigantic watersphere where dolphin technology and dream power converge. Inside the aquatic globe, dolphin astronauts program a mighty supercomputer with ultrasonic commands. However, maverick dolphin Abacus develops his own agenda and accelerates far beyond human intelligence."[25] The summary hints at the preconscious, almost hallucinogenic tones of the script. At the center of the Bluestar watersphere is Illiad, the artificial superintelligence realized through "hydraulic computing," who also acts as a dolphin translator by visualizing cetacean mental states through holograms called "dream beams."[26] This space station was an architectural typology created to accommodate and amplify multiple types of intelligent entities. As the screenplay unfolds, Illiad and Abacus become confidants and, ultimately, coconspirators. Merging into a kind of animal-AI superconsciousness, they attempt to found "a new history of Delphic civilization," creating startling hallucinations of human history subjugated by dolphins.[27] With the dolphin-AI symbiosis complete, the new hybrid superintelligence has a message for humans: "Delphic knowledge extends far beyond human perception. And believe me, we are on the threshold of a dynamic future."[28]

The screenplays for *Bluestar* and *Brainwave* presented an unusual framing for computational media, one that emphasized communication not only between humans, or between humans and machines, but also between humans and animal or alien intelligences. They make a case for the role of a computer as translator between highly disparate agents and modes of expression. The possibilities hinted at in these screenplays, outlandish though they may have initially appeared, have only become more viable in the intervening decades. Today, some AI researchers are optimistic about the application of neural networks to translate animal utterances, including cetacean translation.[29] Perhaps our 21st-century iteration of the Dolphin Embassy is lurking just around the corner.

Beyond technologically mediated interactions between humans, artificial intelligence, animals, and the environment that they depicted, *Brainwave* and *Bluestar* were also pretexts

24. Ibid., 32.
25. *Bluestar: Man is the Dream of the Dolphin* (Bluestar Productions, 1991).
26. Ibid., 29, 138.
27. Ibid., 162, 164.
28. Ibid., 164–65.
29. Jacob Andreas, Gašper Beguš, Michael M. Bronstein et al., "Cetacean Translation Initiative: a roadmap to deciphering the communication of sperm whales," https://doi.org/10.48550/arXiv.2104.08614 (arXiv:2104.08614).
30. Michels and Shannon, "The Humans: Synopsis," 4.
31. Ant Farm, Enviroman (Ant Farm Timeline), 11 by 8 1/2 inches, University of California, Berkeley Art Museum and Pacific Film Archive (2005.14.1.12).
32. Michels and Shannon, "The Humans: Synopsis," 2.

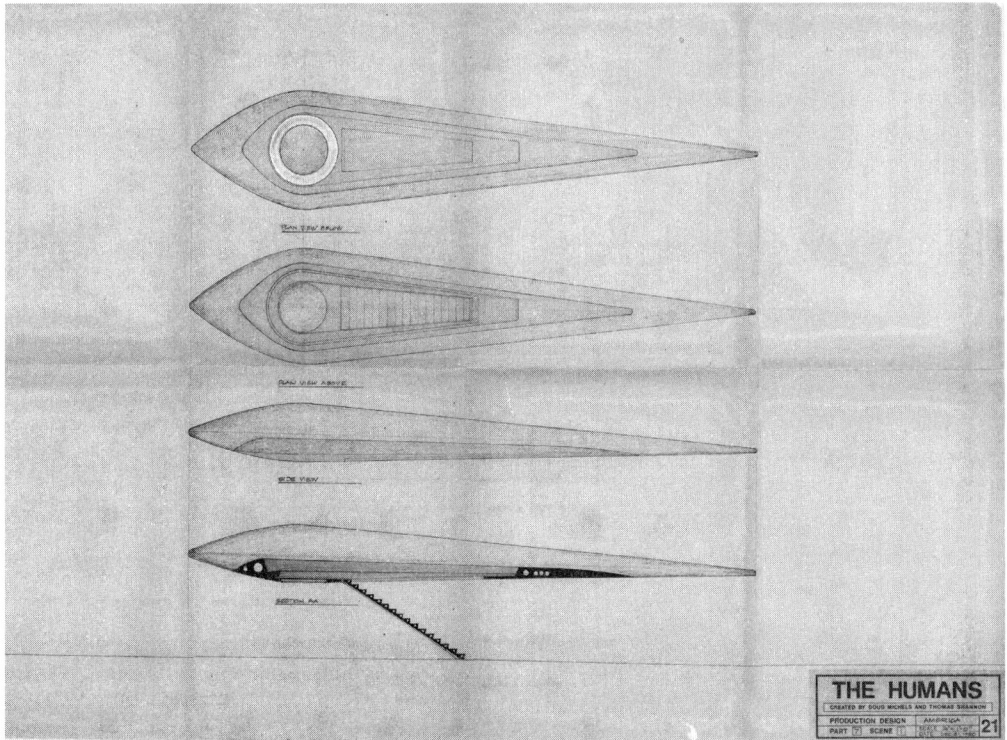

An enigmatic unnamed craft from the production design of "The Humans," evidently with a large conversation pit for passengers. It oddly evokes the craft of the 1986 film *Flight of the Navigator*. Doug Michels and Thomas Shannon, "The Humans: Precis" (unpublished manuscript, June 10, 1980).

to imagine how communications technologies could reorganize a posthuman domestic life. The embassy was, after all, a place where humans lived long-term, ideally in close proximity with cetaceous companions. "The Humans," too, presented swim tanks in which dolphins and humans might form new relationships, alliances, and bonds.[30] For Ant Farm and Michels, environment, media, and architecture were interwoven in strange but inextricable assemblages, often altering the sociality of humanity itself. The convolution of humans and the environment through media was exemplified by a new hybrid archetype that Ant Farm named Enviroman: "the man of the future, plugged into an Alpha computer environments [*sic*] of the Howdy Doodey future. Image Technology is born."[31]

Returning full circle to the first scene of "The Humans," inside the massive glass sphere, a planetary press conference unfolds. With a video beamed across the globe to thousands of participants, the conference is an intimation of the effortless and infinitely scalable video calls of today. With a dramatic flourish, the presenter unveils "the total pattern of calls happening at that moment – the rotunda quickly fills with a complex weave of pulsing beams."[32] The architecture of the sphere transforms into a panoramic view of global communication, a planetary ecology of data transactions.

Though this was an opening scene for the film, it is also an apt coda for Michels's film work: an almost recursive embedding of a media pseudo-event within an architecture, nested in a filmic fiction. It distilled the tendencies of Michels's screenplays, with media and architecture fully coinciding, reality and fantasy jostling each other in creative friction. Randy Nakamura's observation about the Dolphin Embassy is equally applicable to many of Michels's film projects: they are "less a literal attempt at an unwieldy fusion of scientific, artistic, and technological research than a method of blurring the boundaries of fact and fiction in order to probe at the boundaries of the human."[33] Those fuzzy human thresholds were particularly challenged by the new digital media of communication and calculation, which could achieve their own autonomy and interact with animals and humans in unpredictable ways. Whether as quasificititious pseudo-events or as overtly fantastic film scripts, for Michels, designed narratives became an extended field of architectural and social speculation that probed the future of media for human and animal users alike. Story, imagination, architecture, and media were woven together in a larger system of imagined worlds and environments for the altered humans of tomorrow.

33. Nakamura, "Architecture, Media, and Technologies," 154.

Andrew Witt is an associate professor in practice at the Harvard Graduate School of Design and a cofounder, with Tobias Nolte, of Certain Measures. His most recent book, *Formulations: Architecture, Mathematics, Culture*, is available from MIT Press.

Observations on a "Midnight Moment"

June 30, 11:56 pm – It's past my bedtime. In the city that never sleeps, I've staked out a good spot in Times Square, near the TKTS seating, to witness artist Marco Brambilla's edition of "Midnight Moment," the nightly digital art exhibition that, since 2012, has featured a different artwork every month. Brambilla – who last year, reimagined Dante's journey through purgatory on the Sphere in Las Vegas – fed images from historic World's Fairs to an AI to create Approximations of Utopia. Over the clamor of tourists and buskers, I hear a cop standing nearby tell his partner, "It's about to start."

11:57 – In unison, the 92 digital billboards that line Times Square from 41st to 49th Street display a film reel countdown. The crowd settles to a murmur, and someone asks, "What's happening?" 3…2…1… Walls of blue sky dotted with clouds form a metaverse in which Superstudio-like grids imply a floor and ceiling. In between, dreamlike, amorphous follies drift by, glitching as they move. I make out Buckminster Fuller's 1967 geodesic dome in Montreal, or maybe it's the 1964 globe in New York. The Atomium, from the Brussels fair in 1958, alchemically transmutes into some Metabolic imaginaries from the 1970 expo in Osaka.

11:58 – Everyone is recording the scene on their phone. I zoom in with mine to see the far end of Times Square, where every New Year's Eve, the crowd celebrates a different midnight moment. The screens display a cascading series of platforms, each carrying variously sized conical pavilions. I don't recognize the World's Fair precedent; perhaps this is a creation of the AI's own utopian imagination.

11:59 – The crowd's attention begins turning back to the buskers, and mine wanders toward

Marco Brambilla, *Approximations of Utopia*, "Midnight Moment," June 1 – June 30, 2024, Times Square, New York. Photo: Patrick Templeton.

late-night anxieties: Did we give up on these utopian dreams, are we content ceding them to AI? Will AI help create a future Eutopia, or will it always be this non-place stuck on the other side of a screen? Does it matter? The group next to me poses for a low-angle selfie with Approximations of Utopia as a backdrop. What is dystopia if not an approximation of utopia?

12:00 – Advertisements burst back on the screens. A polychromatic cloud of makeup for Sephora's Pride campaign replaces Brambilla's sky. To my left, the entire wall is now a smoky, ruinous cityscape for some TV show with the tagline "You can't bury the past." I push my way through the crowd to head home and get some sleep.

– Patrick Templeton

Observations on Desire Paths

Broadway, south of West 27th Street, New York. Photo: Riley Grills.

Call it a social trail, fishermen trail, herd path, buffalo trace, bootleg trail, pirate path, or, as author Robert Macfarlane writes, a "free-will way," a desire path emerges when convenience contradicts a walker's planned route. Often manifesting as a well-trod trail of dirt between prescribed concrete sidewalks or as a line of matted grass cutting through an overgrown field, the route of greater efficiency emerges over time, charting human and animal behaviors and, sometimes, becoming designated paths themselves.

According to urban planners, the oldest desire path in the United States is thought to be Broadway in New York City. Originally known as the Wickquasgeck Trail, the Native American footpath emerged due to its high elevation in the swampland of Manahatta, or "hilly island." This 13-mile artery between Lenape and other Indigenous settlements became the designated route for trade and communication. In the 1620s, Dutch colonists widened the trail and renamed it BredeStraat, meaning "wide street." In 1664, during the British occupation, it was changed to Broadway.

The thoroughfare facilitated two-way traffic, cutting diagonally across the urban grid, until the 1960s when it became one-way southbound below 59th Street. In 2009, the New York City Department of Transportation closed Broadway to vehicular traffic from 42nd to 47th Street to improve urban safety and mobility by establishing pedestrian plazas and bicycle lanes and introducing new public spaces with seating and landscape. As the DOT continues to reinvent more segments of Broadway as slow, shared, or plaza blocks, they produce a new "social trail" – not only a path of desire but also a path to desire.

– Riley Grills

Iman Ansari

Toward a Program Of Action

My office is on the second floor of Knowlton Hall – the architecture school designed by Mack Scogin Merrill Elam Architects for The Ohio State University. The building is organized by a series of long ramps that connect floors, each of which is dedicated to a distinct program: common spaces, offices, studios, and a library. Embedded in this elegant arrangement is yet another programmatic paradigm: the men's and the women's bathrooms are placed at the opposite ends of the building and on alternate floors. When I need to use the bathroom, I have to make a decision: climb two flights up or down or walk across the length of the building via a narrow passageway lined with faculty offices. I could walk to the nearest bathroom, just a few steps away, but then I'd risk being seen in a space designated for "WOMEN." Through this sequence of rooms, doors, corridors, catwalks, ramps, stairs, and signage, every bathroom trip involves either a physical or a social labor – assuming I don't take the elevator or avoid my chatty colleagues.

This subliminal programming is not the functionalism we were taught by the modernists. Something else is at play. Scogin and Elam had a different kind of program in mind when they devised their plan to compel users like me to be more active or collegial. Thus, two distinct types of program are at work in Knowlton Hall: a conventional, passive program that uses language in the form of instructions, labels, and signs (Classroom, Auditorium, Office, Quiet Room, MEN, WOMEN, etc.) to describe the function of spaces; and an active program that utilizes physical elements (rooms, stairs, ramps, corridors, doors, etc.) to prescribe specific user behavior and function. If the former is a *program of narrative*, the latter is a *program of action*.

Despite its efficacy, active programming has been denigrated by social and architectural theorists as a coercive mechanism, a vestige of the disciplinary regime of the 19th century, or a remnant of the social engineering projects of the 20th century.[1] But whereas those projects favored mechanisms of control to subjugate and discipline populations, a program of action invites users to participate in the construction of

1. Since the 1970s, the critique of modern institutional structures by social theorists like Michel Foucault, Henri Lefebvre, and Jürgen Habermas has gone hand in hand with architectural theorists' critique of the deterministic function of program. Manfredo Tafuri challenged modernism's complicity in the capitalist program, Peter Eisenman criticized architecture's shift towards "a social or programmatic art" and negated modernist functionalism altogether, and Colin Rowe called programming "naive scientism." Even Bernard Tschumi, who embraced program, was critical of modern architecture's revolutionary urges to "both reflect and mold the society to come" through the creation of new programs. Manfredo Tafuri, *Architecture and Utopia: Design and Capitalist Development*, trans. Barbara Luigia La Penta (Cambridge: MIT Press, 1976 [Italian edition, 1973]); Peter Eisenman, "Post-Functionalism," *Oppositions* 6 (September 1976): i–iv; Colin Rowe, "Program vs. Paradigm," *Cornell Journal of Architecture* 2 (1982): 8–19; Bernard Tschumi, Architecture and Disjunction (Cambridge: MIT Press, 1996), 114.

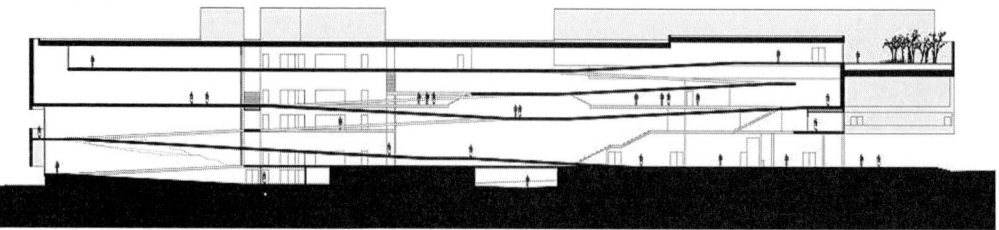

Mack Scogin Merrill Elam Architects, Austin E. Knowlton School of Architecture, The Ohio State University, Columbus, Ohio, 2005. Section through the circulation ramps. Drawing courtesy the architects.

2. Julien Guadet, *Éléments et théorie de l'architecture*, vol. 1 of 4 (Paris: Librarie de la construction moderne, 1909), 1:180.
3. John Summerson, "The Case for a Theory of Modern Architecture," *Journal of the Royal Institute of British Architects* 64, no. 8 (June 1957): 310.
4. Ibid.

social relations and the subjectivities such interactions sanction. A program of action is conceived in the space of interaction between the environment and the individual, taking into account one's behavior, social identity, and physical health and well-being. To embrace a program of action is to consider the environment as a reflexive domain and to reclaim our agency – as authors, architects, or users – in shaping societal dynamics.

Program is a distinctly modern phenomenon. When it entered the curricula of design schools like the École des Beaux-Arts, program denoted both a course of study and a course of action. Julien Guadet's 1909 textbook *Éléments et théorie de l'architecture* describes the architect as "the artist who can execute a program."[2] By establishing a linear relationship between form and function, modernism cast program as an alibi for functionalism. In his 1957 address to the Royal Institute of British Architects, "The Case for a Theory of Modern Architecture," John Summerson hails program as the one unifying principle of modernism. But he also identifies a missing link in the application of program to form: as a set of interdependent conceptual relationships, programmatic ideas resist translation into a comprehensive formal logic. Summerson sees this lack of a program-form technique, a void left by the absence of antiquity's absolute authority, as modernism's "missing architectural language."[3] He dismisses both the purely "rationalist" approach promoted by Reyner Banham and the "geometrical" measures of Le Corbusier's Modulor, which produce systems of "control" rather than "expression." Both approaches, he argues, fail to provide a language. Ending on a pessimistic note, Summerson speculates that "it is quite possible that the missing language will remain missing."[4]

Throughout the 1960s, numerous architects searched for that programmatic language. At a time when computer scientists were developing programs that facilitated human-machine interaction, architects like Cedric Price were exploring new programs that considered architecture as a form of cyber-physical interface. In developing his interactive Fun Palace, Price and cybernetician Gordon Pask merged architectural programming with computer programming to digitally process and transmit user inputs to the architectural and human actors. For the Potteries Thinkbelt, Price repurposed abandoned industrial sites and an existing railway system into an educational network that could transform in response to social and economic fluctuations. He theorized the Thinkbelt's feedback mechanism as "life-conditioning": a flexible and adaptable architecture that, much like a thermostat, would be able to respond to changes in its environment and approximate life's indeterminacy with a degree of "calculated uncertainty."[5] For Price and other architects influenced by cybernetics and systems theories, the computer offered a new framework for rethinking program in architecture, a framework in which the user, more than a passive recipient or mere subject, actively engages in both information exchange and the transformation of the environment.

Life-conditioning, however, came under scrutiny for relegating the architect to the role of a scientist who treated human subjects as mere objects. In 1967, in a scathing critique, George Baird labels Price's Thinkbelt a "servicing mechanism" that – along with Eero Saarinen's CBS Headquarters in New York – stood as a bizarre consequence of the bankrupt traditions of the 19th century and a "loss of faith in rhetoric."[6] For Baird, who saw architecture's fundamental purpose as the production and transmission of meaning, establishing utility as meaning only generated "meaninglessness."[7] Inspired by structuralist and semiological theories, he contended that only a linguistic system could transcend the utilitarian constraints of Saarinen's Gesamtkunstwerk and Price's life-conditioning, ultimately overcoming the form-function dialectic.[8] For him, Summerson's "missing language" appeared to be language itself.

In the decades that followed, the discourse on program was gradually eclipsed by a growing interest in language. The persistent critique of a Benthamesque utilitarian approach, as interpreted from the work of theorists like Michel Foucault and, later, Gilles Deleuze, portrayed active programming as a coercive and inhumane misuse of power that turns architecture into a biopolitical instrument.[9] Meanwhile, the failure of projects like Pruitt-Igoe, demolished in the early 1970s, further dissuaded architects from a programmatic engagement with social issues. Instead, many sought to prioritize language over reductive functionalism, choosing to merely

5. Cedric Price, "Life-conditioning," *Architectural Design* (October 1966): 483.
6. George Baird, "'La Dimension Amoureuse' in Architecture," in *Architecture Theory since 1968*, ed. K. Michael Hays (Cambridge: MIT Press, 1998), 42, 46. Originally published in *Arena: The Architectural Association Journal* 83 (1967). Reprinted in Charles Jencks and George Baird, eds., *Meaning in Architecture* (New York: George Braziller, 1969), 79–99.
7. Ibid., 54.
8. Not everyone agreed with Baird's portrayal. Coming to Price's defense against the "intellectual dead-ends" promoted by structuralists, Banham saw in the Thinkbelt a powerful alternative for the future of architecture: "a nearly value-free" environment, devoid of "other people's values left over from the past," and one that is "capable of generating new values semiotically with its inhabitants." Reyner Banham, "The Architecture of the Wampanoag," in Charles Jencks and George Baird, eds., *Meaning in Architecture* (New York: George Braziller, 1969), 102.
9. See Michel Foucault, *Discipline and Punish: The Birth of the Prison*, trans. Alan Sheridan (New York: Pantheon Books, 1977 [French edition, 1975]); Gilles Deleuze, "A New Cartographer (Discipline and Punish)" in *Foucault*, trans. Seán Hand (Minneapolis: University of Minnesota Press, 1988 [French edition, 1986]), 33.

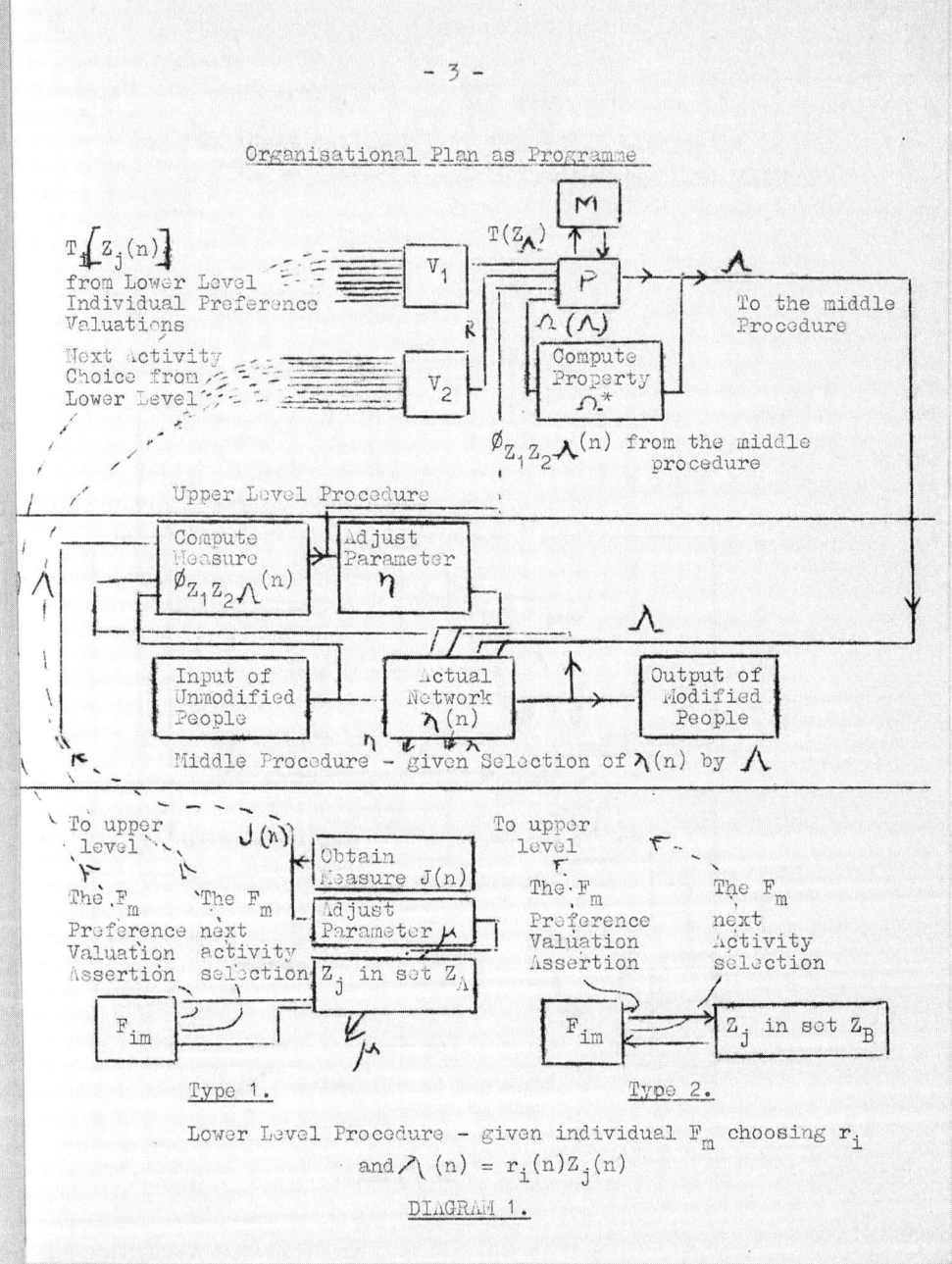

Gordon Pask and Cedric Price, "Organisational Plan as Programme," 1965. From *Minutes of the Fun Palace Cybernetics Committee Meeting, 27th January 1965*. Drawing courtesy the Cedric Price Fonds, Canadian Centre for Architecture, Montreal.

accommodate program, if they acknowledged it at all. Some – including Peter Eisenman, Aldo Rossi, Robert Venturi, and Denise Scott Brown – resisted or even rejected the determinacy of function in favor of an autonomous linguistic system that produced meaning through formal, typological, and semiotic operations. Those who acknowledged program – like John Hejduk, Bernard Tschumi, and Rem Koolhaas – embraced it as a narrative structure with which to compose plots, transcripts, and polemics. Both approaches ultimately coalesced around the diagram, a graphical abbreviation of formal, conceptual, and even programmatic relations that, at least for the time being, appeared to fulfill Summerson's "missing language."

At the heart of Summerson's observation lies the assumption of an irreconcilable difference between program, which is descriptive and textual in nature, and form, which is inherently visual and material. Summerson defines program as a "*description* of the spatial dimensions, spatial relationships, and other physical conditions required for the convenient performance of specific functions," whereas form emerges from the ordering of a vast number of spatial, material, and practical variables into a "visually comprehensible whole."[10] In formulating his conception of program and form, Summerson assumes a distinction between textual *inscriptions* and material *artifacts* in informing social dynamics. Bruno Latour, in his 1992 essay "Where Are the Missing Masses? The Sociology of a Few Mundane Artifacts," questions this distinction.[11] Through an elaborate picture that moves from doors, automated door-closers, hinges, and keys to maps, instructions, signs, labels, and warning messages, Latour illustrates how ordinary inscriptions and artifacts prescribe everyday human actions through a specific "pre-inscription" delegated to them by their authors and designers. He argues that the "missing masses" that account for the balance of society are found not in social constructs or technological systems alone, but in the dynamic space of interaction between the two domains.

To illustrate this, Latour uses the example of a simple key: While it endows the user with the ability to unlock a door, the key does not require the user to open or close and relock the door. Despite various narrative appeals in the form of rules, instructions, and signs, "undisciplined" tenants still forget or neglect to lock their doors, potentially leading to break-ins. To solve the problem, a Berlin locksmith designed a key that could not be removed from the lock without relocking the door. By inscribing a program of action into the shape

10. John Summerson, "The Case for a Theory of Modern Architecture," in *Architecture Culture 1943–1968: A Documentary Anthology*, ed. Joan Ockman (New York: Columbia Books on Architecture/Rizzoli, 2000), 233. Originally published in *Journal of the Royal Institute of British Architects* 64, no. 8 (June 1957): 307–13.

11. Bruno Latour, "Where Are the Missing Masses? The Sociology of a Few Mundane Artifacts," in *Shaping Technology/Building Society: Studies in Sociotechnical Change*, ed. W. E. Bijker, and J. Law (Cambridge: MIT Press, 1992), 225–58.

of the key and the lock, the designer prescribes a specific behavior, translating a potential program of morality into one of "dire necessity." We might then ask: Is the established moral and social order a result of enforcing codes of conduct and responsible human behavior, or does it stem from the prescribed program of action embedded in the key?

The great divide between society – the world of *inscriptions* – and technology – the realm of *artifacts* – is one of the central themes of modernity. This perceived divide, however, overlooks the agency of objects and spaces in shaping our social behaviors and norms. Latour's key insight, more than differentiating between the two domains, is about articulating the dual nature of program itself in negotiating moral codes and social dynamics: while narrative programs remain confined to textual descriptions, programs of action incorporate non-textual elements to enact specific behaviors or functions. This nuance was largely overlooked by Summerson, Banham, Baird, and others who, in their quest for a "missing language," equated programmatic *action* with *narrative* description.

Jeremy Bentham's Panopticon has long embodied a quintessential program of action, one that, through spatial distribution and the application of discipline, sought to correct, educate, reform, and even cure its inmates, "all by a simple idea in Architecture!"[12] Conversely, the Panopticon has also been vilified as the archetypal cautionary tale of the oppressive and coercive power of active programming. Foucault's discussion of Panopticism in *Discipline and Punish* instilled the cynical assumption that modernity is simply a process of subjugation and discipline, one that precludes agency and reduces the individual to an effect or *object* of external conditioning. Yet the key lesson of Foucault's Panopticism is that *biopower*, or the institutional practices that regulate bodies and populations, emanates from both the center and the periphery. The disciplinary diagram, as Sven-Olov Wallenstein observes, is only one aspect of a larger process of simultaneous subjugation and subject formation that constitutes knowledge and power. This process of *assujettissement*, or subjection, in Foucault's terms, reflects the dual nature of power as a phenomenon that shapes individuals both via external forces and through their internal responses to them. Wallenstein describes the mechanisms by which biopower simultaneously constrains individuals *and* enables their self-production as the "technologies of the self."[13] Biopower, then, does not merely operate through discipline but also through self-formation. It is not just an oppressive power *over* but also a productive power *to*.

12. Jeremy Bentham, *Panopticon; Or, The Inspection-House* (Dublin: T. Payne, 1791), 140.
13. See Sven-Olov Wallenstein, *Biopolitics and the Emergence of Modern Architecture* (New York: Princeton Architectural Press, 2009).
14. "Braincoat" from DS+R website https://dsrny.com/project/blur-braincoat.
15. For a treatment of the Blur building along these lines, see Todd Gannon and N. Katherine Hayles, "Virtual Architecture, Actual Media," in *The SAGE Handbook of Architectural Theory*, ed. Hilde Heynen, Stephen Cairns, and C. Greig Crysler (London: SAGE, 2011), 484–500.

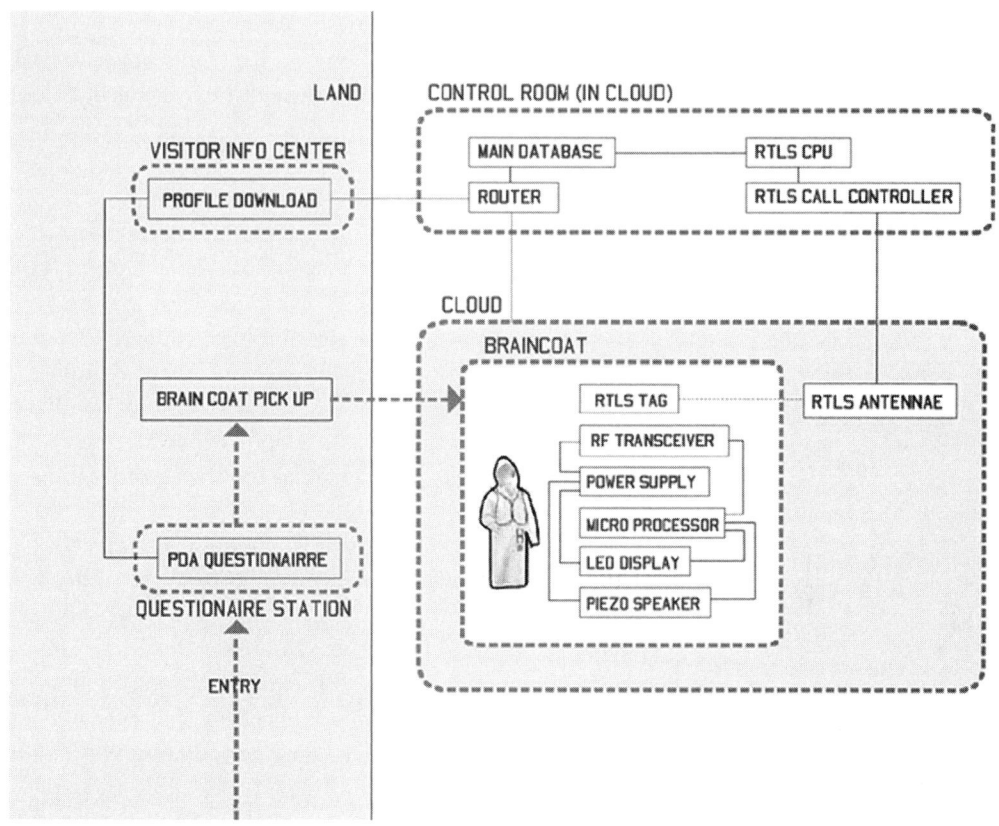

Diller Scofidio + Renfro, Blur Building Brain Coat System Diagram, 2002. Drawing courtesy the architects.

An unlikely example of a program of action that balances the dual nature of biopower is Diller Scofidio + Renfro's Blur Building for the 2002 Swiss Expo. Given the misty form of the pavilion, the architects envisioned the use of a smart raincoat, called a "braincoat," which, in conjunction with a proxy communications network, would function as a "social radar." Visitors were to wear the braincoats after completing a questionnaire, recording their profile data on a transceiver in the coat. As people moved through the mist, the coats would interact by comparing user profiles, triggering colored lights and vibrations that "excite the buttocks" and invite social interaction based on mutual attraction.[14] Building on Price's work, the program of action was embedded in the design of the braincoat in the form of a computer program, allowing architecture to interface the interactions between users and their environment as well as between the users themselves.[15] But most important, the project favored subject formation over subjugation, calibrating the balance between *power-to* and *power-over*.

Acknowledging mechanisms of social- and self-formation involve not a search for a "missing language" but a new *ethics of function.* In 2003, Anthony Vidler called for a new theory of the architectural program that would move beyond the narrow ideological functionalism of early modernism and the revived typological and diagrammatic forms of late modernism. Recognizing that the theorization of a contemporary program lagged seriously behind, Vidler argues for "the radical interrogation of the ethical and environmental conditions of specific sites, which are considered programs in themselves." Such programs, he envisions, while they may not privilege "architecture in the conventional sense," would foster a "new environmentalism" based on what he terms "technologies of the everyday." For Vidler, this programmatic approach would be "flexible and adaptive, inventive and mobile in response to environmental conditions and technological possibilities."[16]

I began writing this essay at Knowlton Hall, traversing the ramps, stairs, and corridors on my trips to the bathroom. A few weeks later, I found myself walking the streets of Tokyo. In the Yoyogi Fukamachi Mini Park, I came across Shigeru Ban's transparent public bathroom, completed in 2020 – one of 17 such facilities designed by renowned Japanese architects and built in the streets and parks of Shibuya Ward as part of "The Tokyo Toilet" project. Ban's colorful glass pavilion sits in the middle of the park, illuminating the space at night. As I approached the structure, I could see the interior through the glass walls and was able to determine whether the space was available, clean, and safe, without having to knock or peek in. Upon entering, as I closed the door behind me and locked it, the transparent walls turned opaque, providing privacy and serving as a reminder to lock the door.[17] When I was done, I left the space as spotless as I had found it because it is always on full display when the walls become transparent again. Ban has prescribed a program of action that translates a biological necessity into a desirable form of social discipline. It operates at both the human scale and the architectural scale. It participates in the formation of individual identities and behaviors as much as it does in maintaining social order. It ensures personal privacy and encourages hygiene just as it contributes to community safety. But most important, it reserves as much agency for city authorities and the architect in shaping social and moral dynamics as it does for individual users.

In response to Summerson's 1957 address, Banham saw the nebulous condition of program in architecture as

16. Anthony Vidler, "Toward a Theory of the Architectural Program" *October* 106 (Autumn 2003): 59–60.
17. For more on this initiative and a catalogue of the projects, see Tami Okano, *The Tokyo Toilet* (Tokyo: Akira Watai, 2023).
18. Reyner Banham, "Discussion," *Journal of the Royal Institute of British Architects* 64, no. 8 (June 1957): 312.

Shigeru Ban Architects, The transparent Tokyo toilet, 2020. Photos: Satoshi Nagare.

emblematic of the rift between theory and practice. He lauded Auguste Choisy for his theoretical prowess in dissolving this dichotomy: "For him, everything good in architecture was determined by pure necessity."[18] Bathrooms epitomize such programs of pure biological and technical necessities, representing architecture's fundamental responsibility to maintain the balance between bodily functions and building requirements. The ongoing debate around unisex bathrooms underscores the fundamentally *architectural* nature of such societal issues, prompting a reevaluation of conventional programs of action to align with contemporary discourses on biology, technology, health, and politics. Yet these issues are not confined to bathrooms alone. Architectural practice is imbued with unspoken rules and tacit norms embedded within spatial relations, as in the mundane mechanics of architectural elements like a door: the direction it swings, where it leads, what it conceals, the gesture required to open it, whether it locks, or whether it is to remain open or closed. Such seemingly banal elements embody programs of action that shape our daily interactions and behaviors in subtle yet profound ways.

Active programming offers a potent mechanism for responding to the complex issues we face today through the latent agency of the objects and spaces we design. Architects have historically maintained a distance from active programming for fear of being coercive. We are taught, even encouraged, to design ostensibly neutral spaces, hoping that by populating our work with labels, figures, and furniture people will use them as we imagine and instruct. We assume that our job is to produce buildings, not behaviors – architects of hardware, not software. But we have also learned, particularly in the past two decades, that discipline is not inherently oppressive or negative; it can also be empowering and positive. Our built environments are already embedded with programs of action whether we consciously devise them or not. To be indifferent to programmatic action and rely on narrative programs and polemics alone is to neglect architecture's profound capacity to condition social values and dynamics.

To embrace a program of action, then, is to reconceptualize our environment as a reflexive domain and to assume agency in shaping societal dynamics in architectural terms. Doing so involves taking a closer look at the small and seemingly insignificant objects and devices that surround us, from the elemental components of buildings to public bathrooms and egress stairs, handrails and wheelchairs, or furniture and fixtures. Beyond passive objects or artifacts of material culture, these standardized devices encode specific social and moral human behaviors that, while singular and local, are also universal and global. To reimagine the interaction between these domains, how we theorize and design them, is to redefine the basic ingredients of architecture as both epistemic and pragmatic *things* and to reprogram the very patterns of everyday life.

Iman Ansari is a founding principal of AN.ONYMOUS and an assistant professor at the Knowlton School of Architecture, The Ohio State University.

Thomas Daniell

Fantastic Voyage

Form and function do not correlate one-to-one, and that is the saving grace of architecture.
— Nanako Umemoto

How are we to understand the surreal forms of the new Kaohsiung Port Terminal at Taiwan's largest and busiest harbor? Designed by New York–based RUR Architecture, the terminal is an asymmetrical knot of tungsten-gray tentacles that somehow eludes easy comprehension of its shape, size, or purpose. As one approaches from the city by automobile or light rail, its profile seems to undulate and writhe, the vermiform appendages slowly extruding and retracting like a multiheaded cobra responding to a celestial snake-charmer. No doubt the effect is similar when arriving by cruise liner or domestic ferry. There is no privileged, definitive viewpoint, no main facade. Lacking conventional fenestration or legible spandrels that would indicate floors, the building's scale is unclear, just as its function is obscured by the lack of distinct programmatic subcomponents and the continuity of the aluminum cladding. The terminal is a virtuoso performance of sculptural modeling that has produced a visually unstable yet iconic architectural form. But an icon of what, exactly? And why here?

In its intimations of life and motion, the terminal has little sense of being anchored in place. Indeed, it gives the impression of having only recently slithered from the sea, its surfaces iridescent in the late afternoon sunlight. The built volume does not appear to be constrained by site boundaries, zoning regulations, or legally defined building envelopes. There is no visible modularity, structural grid, or proportional system, no concessions to human corporeality in scale or detail, no allusions to local history, culture, or context. It even appears relatively unaffected by gravity – a canted tower is counterbalanced by a cluster of cantilevered tubes that lift away from a platform suspended above the waterfront. This raised boardwalk is not a tabletop on which the architecture has simply been placed. The tubes burrow through it from below and spill over its edges, rearing upward and outward

Reiser+Umemoto, RUR Architecture DPC, Kaohsiung Port Terminal, Kaohsiung, Taiwan, 2024. Exiting to the water side of the terminal and onto the public boardwalk. Top: View from the Kaohsiung Harbor. Opposite page: The ramp for vehicular access to drop-off flies over a ground-level entrance. Photos: Iwan Baan.

before being abruptly amputated, even as their presence distorts the surface of the boardwalk itself. From certain angles, the tubes appear vaguely predatory, snuffling trunks searching for airborne prey. Or, more benignly, they recall the effects of tropism, the botanical phenomenon in which plants twist toward sources of light and moisture. Intertwining and interpenetrating, the tubes define small exterior gardens while producing a dynamic play of concave and convex surfaces inside the building.

Indeed, the cavernous interior largely keeps the promise of spatial continuity implied by the enigmatic exterior, though the requirements for privacy, security, and fire safety in an international transport facility have necessitated a few remedial physical and visual barriers – guide ropes, glazed partitions, solid bulkheads – in places where the architects wanted continuity. From the central lobby, one can look through the tubes as they radiate outward and upward, each with a specific destination – boarding gate, harbor-view restaurant, office-tower lobby, observation deck, and so on. Their fully transparent ends are oriented toward the sky, and the partly glazed throats allow views down to the boardwalk and the water beyond. Vertical circulation is mostly hidden within the varying thickness of the building envelope, which conceals a secondary plexus of bundled tubes, some publicly accessible, others for staff and servicing. The result is a Klein-bottle confusion of exterior and interior space through which each visitor is ingested and expelled, like Jonah in the belly of the whale. Or perhaps the passengers should be seen as corpuscles flowing and coagulating though veins, like the miniaturized scientists traversing a human bloodstream in the 1966 film *Fantastic Voyage*.

All these biological analogies may seem overwrought – perhaps the consequence of an architectural object that acts as a Rorschach Inkblot Test for the mental projections of a dazzled critic – but it is worth remembering that the opposition of form and function (in Aristotelian terms, *morphē* and *ergon*) was at the heart of ancient debates on the nature of living things, as well as early 19th-century proto-evolutionary theory, notably the Cuvier-Geoffroy debate, a prolonged argument on questions of morphology and teleology between naturalists Georges Cuvier and Étienne Geoffroy Saint-Hilaire that took place at the Académie Royale des Sciences, in 1830.[1] Cuvier used architectural analogies to argue that natural form follows function – behavioral changes will lead to changes in the relevant body parts – while Geoffroy argued the opposite.[2] The

1. See Paula Young Lee, "The Meaning of Molluscs: Leonce Reynaud and the Cuvier-Geoffroy Debate of 1830, Paris," *Journal of Architecture* 3, no. 3 (Autumn 1998).
2. See David Adams, "The Form-Function Relationship in Architecture and Nature: Organic and Inorganic Functionalism," in Rudolf Steiner, *Architecture, Sculpture, and Painting of the First Goetheanum* (Spencertown, New York: SteinerBooks, 2017).

3. See Johann Wolfgang von Goethe, *Goethe's Botanical Writings*, ed. and trans. Bertha Mueller (Honolulu: University of Hawaii Press, 1952).

4. Gehry's attraction to fish shapes is explained in Calvin Tomkins, "The Maverick," *New Yorker* (June 29, 1997): 38–45, and FOA's exploitation of the wave metaphor is described in Alejandro Zaera-Polo, "The Hokusai Wave," *Perspecta* 37 (2005): 78–85.

5. "There was no question that Wright, Garnier, Loos, Behrens, Gropius were the initiators of the style of the century and that Gaudí and Sant'Elia were freaks and their inventions fantastical rantings." Nikolaus Pevsner, *Pioneers of Modern Design: From William Morris to Walter Gropius* (London: Pelican Books, 1960), 5.

latter position was endorsed by Goethe, who coined the word *morphology* for the study of form in animals and plants, though admittedly in a manner more descriptive than explanatory.[3]

Designed in 2013 and completed in 2022, the terminal seems at first glance to be a nostalgic echo of the enthusiasm for "emergent" forms that characterized the architectural avant-garde of the 1990s, which saw a shift away from the angular disjunctions and fragmentations of deconstructivism toward curvilinear distortions and differentiations within an organic continuity. Indeed, Kaohsiung has apparent precedents in, or at least resonances with, two pioneering waterfront projects from the turn of the millennium: Frank Gehry's Guggenheim Museum Bilbao (1997) and FOA's Yokohama International Passenger Terminal (2002). While Bilbao and Yokohama both use a language of fluid shapes and distorted surfaces – the glittering skin of the former evoking a school of fish, the undulating planes of the latter alluding to ocean waves[4] – their final compositions were arrived at from radically opposed directions. Bilbao comprises arbitrary sculptural profiles imposed on an initial planning schema of orthogonal blocks, whereas Yokohama is an array of interwoven, programmed surfaces extrapolated from an abstract circulation diagram. These two precedents exemplify the extremes of the form-versus-function dichotomy: the intuitive whims of the architect as artist versus the precise delineation of structure and activity by the architect as technician, respectively. Of course, these are not distinct categories but rather positions on a compositional spectrum across which every architect oscillates, more or less widely, from project to project. Kaohsiung seems to have it both ways, manifesting an exuberant expressionism that cannot be fully explained as either formalist or functionalist, but with a foot in each camp.

At least since the birth of modern architecture, expressionism has had a bad reputation, its tendency toward the amoeboid and the crystalline regarded as unjustifiably expensive, indulgent, and unserious in comparison to the sober boxes of mainstream modern architecture. The early 20th-century expressionist architects – primarily Germans such as Erich Mendelsohn, Hermann Finsterlin, Hans Poelzig, Hans Scharoun, and Hugo Häring – tended to be dismissed by historians of the period, notably Nikolaus Pevsner,[5] as decadent aberrations from the lineage of modernism. A reevaluation by Reyner Banham complicated the two approaches by suggesting that expressionism and modernism

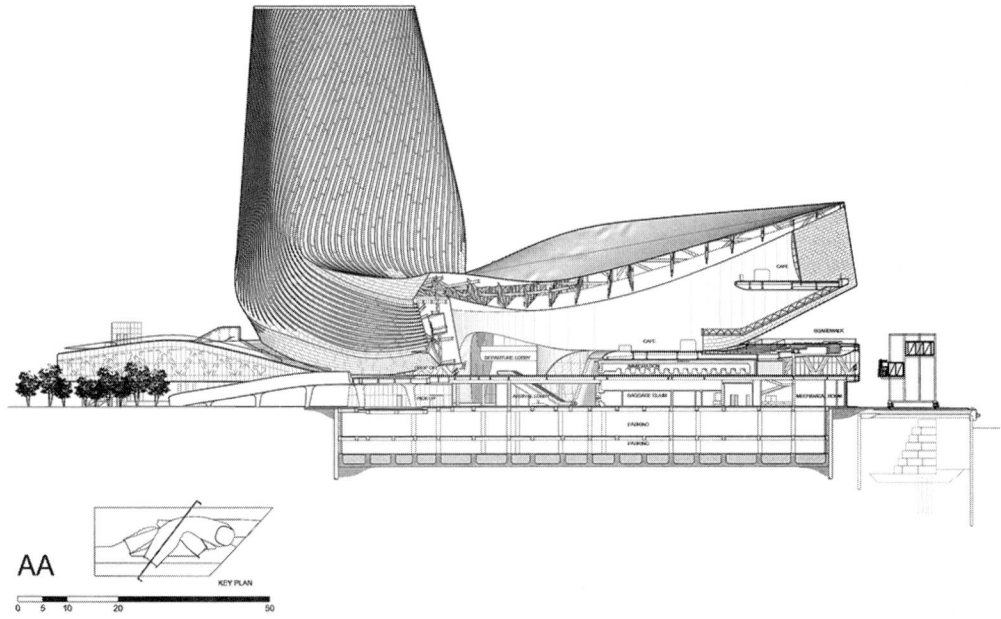

AA

The entrance to the departure hall. Photo: Iwan Baan. Top: Cross section through the primary "lobe," showing the multilevel interchange between civic and maritime public spaces. Drawing courtesy the architects.

had far more in common than either would have liked to admit: "Since the expression of the function of the building is taken to be one of the touchstones of the non-Expressionist approach, we may suspect that we see here, as in so much twentieth-century architectural polemics, one of those situations where an aesthetic standpoint is defended by accusing the other party of abandoning a theoretical position that is, in fact, common ground to both sides."[6] Undoubtedly, modernist orthogonality was all too often romantically and aesthetically motivated, and expressionist plasticity was, in many cases, a rational attempt to make form truly follow function.

During the 1920s, the theoretical and practical implications of this debate were being rehearsed in the Berlin office shared by Ludwig Mies van der Rohe and Häring. For Mies, the best way to contain any function was the loose fit of an oversized, sublimely empty box – or, in his terms, a box filled with "universal space." Häring, by contrast, advocated architectural form that was precisely tailored to the activities it contained and inflected by the specificities of its surroundings. In Adolf Behne's *The Modern Functional Building*, a 1926 survey of German modern architecture, Häring's work is categorized not as expressionist but as the supreme exemplar of "organic functionalism."[7] To be sure, Häring may have rejected Mies's dogged insistence on orthogonal regularity, but he did not insist on replacing it with curvilinear, diagonal irregularity:

The new technique, which works with light constructions, with elastic and supple materials, no longer demands that buildings be rectangular and cubic, but permits or realizes any form which the house as an organ of habitation might suggest. This does not mean that there can no longer be rectangular rooms in a house: certainly not. It means only that rectangularity is not the determinant of the form, that the rectangle appears only as the form of performance-fulfillment, which is something else entirely. . . . In organ-like Gestalt-formation the rectangle is a technical figure, and the geometry is there only as a tool.[8]

With the introduction of parametric software to architectural design in the mid-1990s, it seemed that the latent ambitions of 1920s organic functionalism – an architectural aesthetic predicated on the precise morphological registration of program and context, behavior and climate – might be fully realized. This possibility was adumbrated in Greg Lynn's landmark Folding in Architecture edition of *AD*, in 1993,[9] and then comprehensively articulated in Patrik

6. Reyner Banham, *Theory and Design in the First Machine Age* (New York: Frederick A. Praeger Publishers, 1960), 184.
7. See Adolf Behne, *The Modern Functional Building*, trans. Michael Robinson (Santa Monica: The Getty Research Institute for the History of Art and the Humanities, 1996).
8. English translation from Peter Blundell Jones, *Hugo Häring: The Organic Versus the Geometric* (Stuttgart & London: Axel Menges, 1999), 85–86.
9. See Greg Lynn, ed., *AD 63*: Folding in Architecture (1993), in particular Lynn's compelling introductory essay, "Architectural Curvilinearity: The Folded, the Pliant and the Supple": 8–15.
10. See Patrik Schumacher, *The Autopoiesis of Architecture, Volume 1: A New Framework for Architecture* (London: John Wiley & Sons, 2010), and *The Autopoiesis of Architecture, Volume 2: A New Agenda for Architecture* (London: John Wiley & Sons, 2012).
11. Patrik Schumacher, "Formalism and Formal Research," *ARKETIPO* 104 (July/August 2016): 12–17.
12. Hugo Häring, "Problems of Art and Structure in Building," trans. Peter Blundell Jones, *9H* 7 (1985): 73–82.

An entrance from the water side of the public boardwalk. Photo: Iwan Baan.

Schumacher's two-volume manifesto *The Autopoiesis of Architecture*, in the early 2010s.[10] Schumacher asserts that form does not necessarily follow function, but it does "deliver" function: "Form is the discipline's *internal reference*, i.e. our immediate responsibility, and function is the discipline's *external reference*, i.e. our ultimate responsibility to society mediated via our production of forms."[11] The ideal, albeit impossible, aim would be buildings that emerge as manifestations of an equilibrium between internal, programmatic pressures and external, contextual pressures, avoiding geometric or stylistic preconceptions and thereby producing forms that might be metaphorically understood as having unfurled from a choreographic diagram or coalesced in a long-exposure photograph.

Attempts to optimize architectural form so as to accommodate function lead to the biomorphic or geomorphic, not as the direct mimesis of natural forms, but as the outcome of analogous processes that produce visually similar results. Häring frequently used the example of aircraft: "The form of the aircraft is invented through observing nature, it is the form of performance-fulfillment, thus organ-like and ungeometric. There are people who would place the machine as a geometrical or mathematical performance, and who would therefore consider it the crowning achievement of geometrical culture. This idea seems to me quite wrong. The machine is a creature of organ-like nature."[12]

For Jesse Reiser, who in 1986 cofounded RUR Architecture with Nanako Umemoto, aircraft were also an inspiration even before he thought of making a career in architecture. As a boy making plastic model airplanes, he was already intuiting that the elegance and dynamism of wing

Aerial view of the trilobe terminal and tower. Photo: Iwan Baan.

profiles and airfoil cross sections were a logical consequence of the requirements for aerodynamic lift, implemented through the optimization of form and minimization of materials.[13] This passion for crafting experimental forms has always guided the work of RUR. By the 1990s, RUR was part of a loose group of similarly minded designers and theorists – including Lynn, FOA, and UNStudio – who briefly merged into a working partnership, called United Architects, for the purpose of entering the 2002 World Trade Center design competition. But unlike many of their peers, Reiser and Umemoto have always resisted ceding design decisions to parametric software. The RUR method prioritizes handmade drawings and models, usually in ink and modeling wax, thereby producing building profiles that are concatenations of elliptical and straight line segments connected at tangent points rather than calculus-based continuous variation. Admittedly, at Kaohsiung the hand-modeled forms have been resolved with scripting software to produce the nonstandard gradations of panels and apertures – scales and ridges, gills and pores – that characterize the building envelope.

The spatial organization of the terminal is predicated on a trilobe diagram, which first appeared in RUR's 1994 competition entry for the Cardiff Bay Opera House, then again in the design for their Taipei Music Center, completed in 2020 (and its origins can be traced back to Konstantin Melnikov's

Rusakov Workers' Club of 1928). The Taipei Music Center was to have comprised three distinct buildings integrated by a distended, suspended plaza between them, but changing circumstances and the inevitable compromises made during the eight years of design and construction diluted the trilobe connection so as to make it relatively imperceptible. A more instructive comparison to the Kaohsiung Port Terminal may be made with another recent project in Taiwan, OMA's Taipei Performing Arts Center (2022), a trilobe composition in which three distinct auditoriums – a sphere, a cube, and a wedge – are somewhat brutally embedded in the central rectilinear volume.[14] Both designs comprise abstract, hermetic forms for which a relatively small change in viewing angle causes significant changes in appearance, not only proportional distortions, but also distinctly different profiles. In contrast to the deliberately exacerbated collisions between primary geometries in the OMA project, RUR's terminal is seemingly generated from a pluripotent tube that has been coaxed into stretching and branching along the length of the waterfront site.

If the terminal is understood metaphorically as an organism, it seems more likely to be an invasive exotic species than a native plant occupying its proper ecological niche. But arguably, a comprehensive detachment from context and locality is entirely appropriate to an international transport terminal. Such facilities are less a part of their host cities than they are nodes in a global network of air and sea travel. After passport control, one enters an ambiguous zone where local laws begin to recede – most mundanely in duty-free shopping – then one crosses the threshold into an invisible, extraterritorial maritime corridor that slices across Taiwanese territorial waters before reaching the comity of the open sea. In this sense, the tubes of the terminal should be read not as truncated but as passing through portals into another dimension, the terminal's sinuous silhouette not an incomplete, imbalanced fragment but the visible manifestation of something much larger. The form delivers, yet exceeds, its function, instantiating a more or less frictionless diagram of local flows while symbolically gesturing toward far-flung places. Simultaneously marking and transcending its location, smoothly unifying and differentiating its programmatic components, enchanted and enchanting, the Kaohsiung Port Terminal recalls those mysterious, alien creatures to be found at the curlicued borders of medieval maps: *hic sunt dracones* (here be dragons).[15]

13. "In 1963, an F101-B Voodoo model kit flew into my hands, and it forever transported me into the strange world of model making." Jesse Reiser, "Voodoo," *Log* 50: Model Behavior (Fall 2020): 103.
14. See Kwang-Yu King, "Project Taipei," *Log* 55 (Summer 2022): 57–65.
15. Amusingly, two of the oldest-known terrestrial globes, the Ostrich Egg Globe (circa 1504) and the Hunt-Lenox Globe (circa 1508), place this phrase on the east coast of Asia at the approximate longitude of Taiwan.

Thomas Daniell is a professor of architecture at Kyoto University. His most recent book is *An Anatomy of Influence*.

Observations on a Tower

A Link5G tower at Mulberry and Bayard Streets in New York City's Chinatown neighborhood. Photo: Stanley Spence.

"It's a business model that doesn't work," says a contact at Intersection, the media and technology company that owns approximately 70 percent of CityBridge, the self-described "consortium of leading experts in technology" with the contract to install 5G towers in New York City. CityBridge has promised to primarily deliver 5G service to the city's "internet deserts" in the Bronx, Queens, Brooklyn, and above 96th Street in Manhattan, where over 30 percent of residents have no internet, let alone broadband service. But the towers have been called ungainly, even ugly. Early installation in Manhattan's Upper East Side, Upper West Side, and West Village faced quick and well-funded backlash from powerful neighborhood associations that argued that the towers, which are 32 feet tall and 34 inches in diameter, disfigure the fabric of their historic neighborhoods. For now, installation has ceased citywide, thanks to this community organization.

Masamichi Udagawa and Sigi Moeslinger, who lead Antenna Design, a firm known for its kiosk design, began working for Intersection in 2014, when they won a design competition for a new New York City payphone that would never be built. Since then, they've done a lot of work for the city. According to the contact at Intersection, the city prefers a long-term contract with one firm. This is evident in Antenna's growing portfolio, which includes MetroCard vending machines, MTA emergency intercoms and info stations, and the LinkNYC and Link5G towers, among other projects. Why, then, is the tower so disliked? Do the structural and technical requirements for its height and width preclude good design? Mark Fraser, the city's chief technical officer, has said that a redesign is possible and a public competition may be held. Given the precedent, one wonders if the winner would enter the next long-term relationship with the city.

– Stanley Spence

Kristine Chung

On Bell Towers And Cell Towers

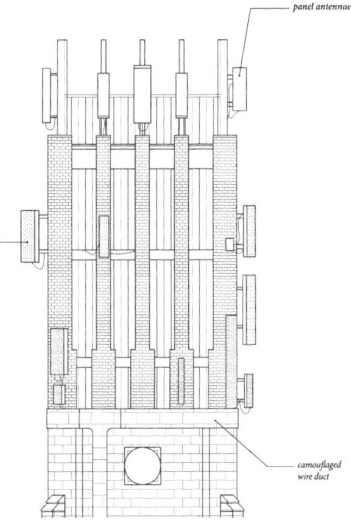

Kristine Chung, Methodist Episcopal Church, Newton, Massachusetts. Bell/cell tower detail. All drawings courtesy the author.

The invisible highway of phone, text, and data signals that enables our communication operates in a surprisingly physical way. While the weightless and shapeless information might seem immaterial (as in the word *wireless*), the transmission of information requires tangible footholds to support a continuous network of antennae, elevated 50 to 200 feet above the ground. Wireless providers, in need of constantly expanding their networks, have developed a curious strategy of camouflaging and grafting to seamlessly permeate the built environment. One form of this parasitism involves hiding cell towers inside church steeples and bell towers, a seemingly perfect symbiosis between old churches that need financial stability and cell towers that need height. And while the appearance of this unlikely union might seem utilitarian or haphazard, every detail, veneer, and joint is a direct consequence of the invisible legal scaffolding around it.

A fascinating example is the former Methodist Episcopal Church, at 288 Walnut Street, in Newton, Massachusetts. Towering over Interstate 90, this church seems utterly typical at a glance: the building consists of a gabled main volume and a square bell tower at the front, veneered with seam-face granite.[1] Looking closely, however, the bell tower appears to be wearing a hat made of a lighter-hued brick with a more contemporary look. Metal poles with box-shaped antennae poke out of the top, and a dozen more antennae are attached to the tower walls, camouflaged with various faux-brick and masonry veneers. Thirty-six antennae are visible on the tower, along with a wiring duct, also camouflaged in masonry veneer. In other words, while the bell tower looks like a historic monument, it is a cell tower hiding in plain sight.

How did this bell/cell tower come to be? Originally built for the Newtonville Methodist Church, in 1861, and refashioned in the Gothic Revival style by Woodbury & Stevens, in 1924, the building served as the main worship space for the congregation until it merged with another church in the area and moved to a different location, in 1980.[2] The building has since had a rather complicated afterlife. After sitting vacant, the church was acquired for commercial purposes, in 1983,

1. "*Newtonville Methodist Church*," 1982, NWT.2431, Massachusetts Historical Commission. Entry by Kim E. Lovejoy, preservation consultant for Ahearn-Schopfer & Associates, P. C. Accessed through MACRIS: Massachusetts Cultural Resource Information System.
2. Ibid.

The former Methodist Episcopal Church, Newton, Massachusetts, seen from Interstate 90. Photo: Stanley Spence, 2024.

and the sanctuary was transformed into Weylu's Chinese restaurant.[3] When the restaurant went bankrupt, in 1986,[4] the sanctuary was once again abandoned, leaving the tower in such poor condition that, in 1992, the City of Newton declared it unsafe.[5] Despite the Newton Historical Commission's objections, the owner truncated the belfry, in 1993,[6] and replaced it with an addition by architect Jeffry Pond,[7] onto which the 36 antennae have been subsequently added. On the City of Newton's online tax database, the building use is categorized as "telecommunications," and the building occupancy is currently registered as "vacant."[8]

While this complicated history may portray the tower as an accidental exquisite corpse, it is nonetheless a carefully constructed artifact in which law and architecture mutually shape each other. Two intentional peculiarities about the tower corroborate this reciprocity: the veneering of antennae and the placement of antennae outside the tower.

The obsessive yet inconsistent veneering of the antennae and wire ducts is the result of a legal mandate to camouflage the facility, a strategy of invisibility typically employed to reduce local resistance.[9] Court cases argued in the aftermath of the Telecommunications Act of 1996[10] have resulted in increased attention to aesthetics. The act mandates that local zoning and planning authorities disregard any claims regarding environmental effects of transmissions and that they not prohibit the provision of personal wireless services.[11] Thus, the only substantive argument on the local communities' side is the aesthetic compliance of the cell towers. In order to secure new tower sites, cell providers must prove to local planning boards that the proposed cell sites are not a

3. Rachel Layne, "Tower Coming Down," *Newton Tab*, May 25, 1993. Photocopy accessed through Historic Newton's archives.
4. "*Newtonville Methodist Church*," 1987, NWT.3640, Massachusetts Historical Commission. Entry by Candace Jenkins and Susan Abele from Newton Historical Commission. Accessed through MACRIS: Massachusetts Cultural Resource Information System.
5. Layne, "Tower Coming Down."
6. This partial demolition is documented by Boston Building Consultants. The existing and proposed elevation drawings, dated October 1, 1992, survive in Historic Newton's archives.
7. Rachel Layne, "Tower Redesign Protested," *Newton Tab*, November 23, 1993.
8. City of Newton Accessor's Database, https://newtonma.mapgeo.io/datasets/properties.
9. For an example of the conflicts that arise between cellular service providers and local zoning and planning boards, see *T-Mobile v. Town of Barnstable*, 969 F.3d 33 (1st Cir. 2020).
10. Telecommunications Act of 1996, Pub. L. No. 104-104, 49 Stat. 1526 (1996), https://www.govinfo.gov/app/details/PLAW-104publ104.
11. These are two of the five restrictions on the local communities' right to deny the application for a new cell site in the Telecommunications Act, U.S.C. § 332 (c)(7)(B).

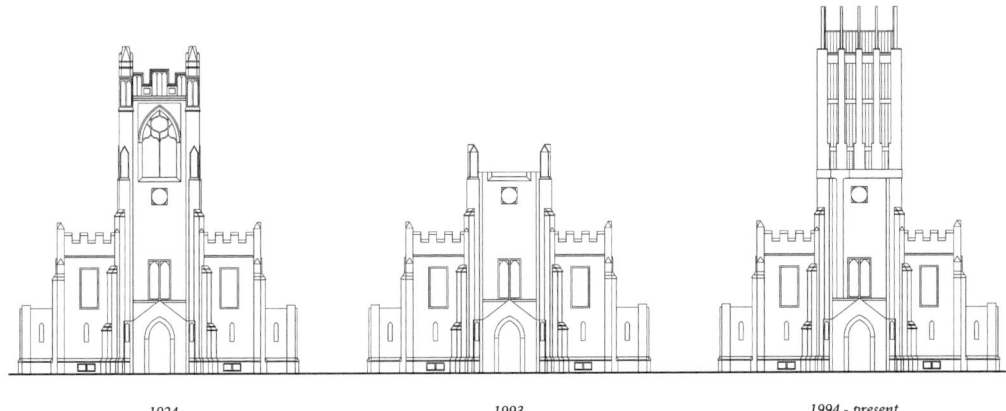

1924　　　　　　　　　　1993　　　　　　　　　1994 - present

Kristine Chung, Methodist Episcopal Church, facade iterations.

12. A common property question around church cell towers revolves around the tax-exempt status of religious buildings, contradicting the property tax implication of cell towers as revenue-generating capital. Since this specific church is no longer used for the original religious purpose, it circumvents this religious tax-exemption conundrum, which allows us to examine the legal consequence of architecture in isolation. For further discussion on the tax-exempt matter, see Judith Lohman, *Taxing Churches Whose Steeples Are Used for Cell Phone Antennas* (Connecticut General Assembly, Office of Legislative Research: August 2001), www.cga.ct.gov/2001/rpt/2001-R-0619.htm.
13. For a discussion on the dual or ambiguous status of cell towers as public goods and private enterprises, see *New Jersey Turnpike Authority v. Elizabeth City*, No. 004383-2014 & 013888-2015 (Tax Court of New Jersey Feb. 10, 2017).

visual nuisance. This has given rise to several peculiar cell towers hidden in fake water towers, cacti, trees, or flag poles, and to adapting existing structures for height. Seen in this light, the faux-brick veneering on the antennae at 288 Walnut Street constitutes a legal argument: provided that wireless carriers can prove their effort to not create an aesthetic anomaly, neither the local community nor the local government can object to the appropriation of a historic landmark. The degree of emulation or consistency of the veneering is secondary because, in the eyes of the law, the intent of aesthetic assimilation is the substance of the argument, not the quality of its execution. As a result, the hues, textures, and scale of the brick and masonry veneering patterns vary wildly, creating a distinctive patchwork, like a glitch in the architectural context.

If camouflaging is such an important legal argument, why are the antennae then placed outside and not more carefully integrated with the tower?[12] Cell towers occupy an ontological gray area with many dual and contrasting identities. They take up a lot of land and real estate for just a few antennae and their supporting equipment. They are seen as a public good, essential for the functioning of our society, yet they are the private property of private companies that provide exclusive service to paying customers.[13] In this legal and architectural ambiguity, it is favorable for wireless providers to declare and demarcate cell towers as *not architecture* and, by extension, *not real property* to avoid legal and tax implications. And this distancing from architecture is construed, ironically, by the architectural details that signal their legal intentions of function and impermanence. The placement of the antennae outside and the rather crude method of affixing the antennae to the bell tower are thus both intentional. Placing the antennae outside circumvents the gray area of counting the occupiable interior square footage of the tower as part of the cell tower. If they were placed inside, property law would treat the wireless providers as rent-paying "tenants," increasing the overall property value of and taxation on the building. Affixing the antennae on separate metal hardware, similarly, is a distancing strategy to establish antennae as temporary fixtures (personal property) as opposed to a permanent improvement (real property). While the boundary between personal and real property is somewhat vague, court cases have again focused on declared intent. If the equipment is clearly dismountable, and if the removal or absence of the equipment leaves no permanent trace on the architecture, cell companies and landlords can argue their legal impermanence, despite the permanence of their decade-long leases.

Strange as they are, parasitic cell towers are not confined to one regulative or legal certainty but span many ambiguities. Although they could be construed radically differently under different legal arguments, these legal subtleties and nuances produce real architectural differences in the built environment. By design, the legal system and the courts are bound to favor demonstrated care and articulated intent. In the absence of a clear verbal or textual representation of its intent, architecture can only be compliant with and disciplined by the legal scaffolding around it. But for the built environment to be designed with intention, this disparity needs to be questioned and the causal relationship reciprocated.

Kristine (Sungyeon) Chung is a Korean Swedish designer. She holds a master of architecture from the Harvard Graduate School of Design. She has practiced and researched with TenBerke, Neri&Hu, and Johnston Marklee. Special thank you to Lisa Haber-Thomson for her mentorship and support.

Christopher Pierce

Cabin Fever

I'm a sucker for Scandinavia. Especially Norway. Transport me into the middle of that typically verdant landscape, dotted with red iron oxide and white painted timber buildings, and all my urban, experimental pretensions are unmasked. It happened again in January, so this time it was the other season's face, the iridescent white one, that welcomed my partner, Dorotea, and me. By the time we exited at the next to last stop on the Oslo Metro T1 line, teeming with children toting their snacks and sleds, I was the closest I'll ever come to attempting a rendition of Johnny Mathis's "Winter Wonderland." The altitude, setting sun, shimmering lights, and cross-country skiers coming at us from every angle made sure that I had none of the steel of London left in me.

I'd made this midwinter trek to see some of Amandine Kastler and Erlend Skjeseth's (Kastler Skjeseth Architects) completed or almost-completed work. I had turned down a chance to troop around with photographer Max Creasy in the fall – a notoriously damp and gray time of year in southern Norway – to wait for winter, the snowy benchmark for assessing any edifice north of 60 degrees longitude. When Erlend called to arrange the next few days, I was wishing I hadn't waited. There was about a meter of fresh snow on the ground, and record-low temperatures were forecast (bottoming out at minus 26 degrees Celsius), making things other than sleeping, sex, and sledding, even for this Viking population, a lot more complicated. The jewel I'd come to see, in Nordmarka (Northern Outback), was apparently inaccessible. How the hell, I thought, am I going to write an article about a log cabin for *Log*, and for which I'd done all the prerequisite reading – everything from Harriet Beecher Stowe to some guy's story about recently building a little cabin in Canada, unimaginatively called *Cabin*? On second thought, I was surrounded by the things. Norway is the global capital of cabin culture.

On our second day in Norway, having eaten elk and played scopas the night before, I made my way to St. Halvardsgate 33 in Oslo's Gamlebyen (Old Town) neighborhood. After trying the door of a yoga studio, I heard Erlend

Kastler Skjeseth Architects' office, Oslo, 2024. Photo: Christopher Pierce.

calling from the window above the Automekanikeren. I should have guessed that their 40-square-meter, two-room office would be perched above a car repair shop. Instead of incense and mindful music, I entered a petrol-infused environment of air screwgun screeching. A certain utility and utilitarianism sum up them both, right down to their shared digs. It was a slow Friday, in the middle of the Norwegian holidays, which gave us a chance to catch up and eat a Danish-influenced sandwich that Norwegians call a *smørbrød*. We also spent about 30 minutes in front of a computer screen, toggling through a wide array of Amandine and Erlend's recent work. The conversation speedily veered from a peculiar photo of an in situ stone "stuck" in white polystyrene at their unfinished cabin in Sponvika to a patterned elevation drawing of Robert Venturi and Denise Scott Brown's Fire Station # 4 (1968) as a potential solution to the Sponvika conflict. I immediately liked the surprise of Erlend referencing one of architecture's classic couples. Around us, the studio is lined with floor-to-ceiling stock steel shelving filled with models. They aren't dollhouse models, much less precious "artifacts," as Amandine and Erlend call them, but volumes and intersections that only a capital *A* architect would ever bother to make.

In the midst of headline-grabbing collectives, crafters, and collaborations, you'd be forgiven for not noticing a small group of fairly ordinary offices of architects that have sprung up in the UK and Europe and are doing simple and slightly twisted things with buildings, new and old. My real appetite, though, is for when those "ordinary" architects intervene in the existing and don't start from scratch. A tabula rasa is a touch *too* ordinary, particularly at a moment when digging a foundation has been made to feel like murder. It was the London-based architect Takero Shimazaki (t-sa) who first told me that "we don't need to build anymore; we just need to reuse." I'm still hung up on his early 21st-century proclamation and the interest it piqued in me about the work of Belgian architects Jan de Vylder and Inge Vinck, especially when they were practicing with Jo Taillieu. I've got a fetish for de Vylder's Excel drawings (and his Instagram feed in general), but the meatier conversation that de Vylder, Vinck, and Taillieu have brought to the table is how to tackle a dilapidated building. They've since led me to BAST in France, Clancy Moore and Ryan W. Kennihan in Ireland, Bovenbouw in Belgium, and Schneider Türtscher and Valentin Deschenaux in Switzerland, among others. However, all this time I've felt that one office has been missing in the mix. That's Kastler Skjeseth.

Our conversation covered most of these architects as Erlend and I aimed for the Swedish border in the family's secondhand gray Toyota Avensis. An hour or so later, we pulled into the construction site of the new build in Sponvika. A punchy place name for a punchy version of a log cabin going up, which partially made up for missing out on Nordmarka. It was three o'clock, and the low-slung sun was already setting.

Set in a picturesque village of about 500 people, this 73-square-meter elaborate "cabin" seems a bit hodgepodge and ad hoc in its conventional monovolume context, as if it were turned inside and out. It almost mocks its well-mannered neighbors, the landscape, and itself. Amandine and Erlend are good at this sort of architectural dark art. They're overeducated, overthinking students, as Erlend put it, of "disguising an architectural idea as a practical idea." The mesmerizing asymmetries, falsifications, subtle surface manipulations, and visual double entendres in this cabin aren't grammatically part of the vanilla building type typically found in Norway. They also aren't all noticed on first, second, or even third glance. That subtlety (or subterfuge) is the point. The cabin is also kind of constantly checking itself out – which couldn't be more apt in our Insta era. What I mean is, while it's wrapped in an aesthetic envelope that seems essentially in step with everything around it, the building's planimetric ins and outs and sectional ups and downs repeatedly force you to confront it from different positions and perspectives. This includes a ribbon window framing the landscape – which the architects were obliged to provide for the zeros that a glimpse of the Sea of Skagerrak adds to the property value. There are other moments when that same requisite window, with its irregular format, drops to the floor and rises to the ceiling, reminding you that this structure isn't a typical functional rectangle. How many times has a building ever asked you to intentionally stare at its timber cladding or reflect on the underside of its soffit? It's peculiarly satisfying.

For me, a lot of 16th-century Italian mannerist rhetoric resurfaces in this tightly planned and pimped, Swedish-produced, prefabricated glulam structure set on a THERMOMUR EPS foundation capped with a Plannja zinc-magnesium corrugated pitched roof. Kastler Skjeseth uses, challenges, and even weaponizes the standard set of building systems familiar to every Scandinavian builder. In this case, there were three of them – Ole, Jim Andre, and Jonny

Right and opposite page: Kastler Skjeseth Architects, Sponvika Cabin (aka Hilltop Cabin), Halden, Norway, completed June 2024. Photos: Louis Gervais. All drawings courtesy the architects.

– solving the puzzle. It's a comparatively poor man's Giulio Romano challenging contemporary Norwegian conceptions of grammar, space, and gutters – two of three things that Venturi obsessed about years ago at the American Academy in Rome – in less ideal and idealistic circumstances. At the time of my visit, the conundrum was resolving the EPS surface with the stone stuck in it. That's when Kastler Skjeseth turned to the visual playbook of Venturi, Scott Brown, and particularly to how they graphically divided exterior surfaces in the '70s.

The Sponvika cabin's surface and orthogonal restlessness made me think of one of Kastler Skjeseth's first projects, which I visited at the time of its completion, in 2018, on Lyngør Island, off Norway's southern coast. In some ways less subtle, but an equally astute "building as cultural commentator," the 80-square-meter Bryggerhus – basically a storehouse – is detached from, but in service of, the 300-square-meter Doktorhus, on which they cut their teeth in 2017. The Doktorhus is a little too

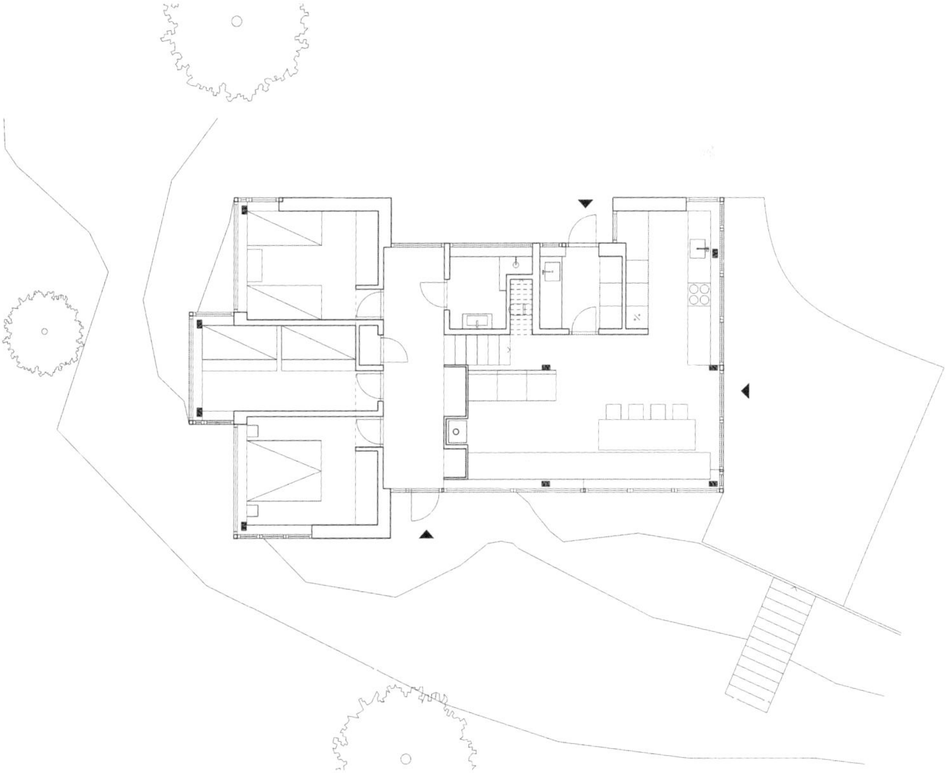

Kastler Skjeseth Architects, Bryggerhus, Lyngør Island, Norway, 2018. Photos: Erlend Skjeseth.

David-Chipperfield-meets-Norwegian-culture-via-a-rich-Brit-client for my taste. Next door, however, the architects took the "runt" of the three-building site, a fairly unassuming, 18th-century notched-log construction clad with timber panel, and repaired it, painted the exterior entirely white, and then, by Norwegian standards, went full throttle on the interior. Through an unassuming door, you enter a world of applied colors, patterns, and textures that aren't as culturally alien as the majority of the Norwegian population thinks and that elevate notched-log construction to another aesthetic level.

In that context, Kastler Skjeseth are distinct from offices that are more palatable and publishable in a grainy, *AMAG*-reserved kind of way. I don't think it's only their youth or their client base. It's an ingrained sardonic side that helps their work be real, witty, and relevant. In other words, it wasn't only the air that was refreshing. The legitimacy of their smaller projects is in what Erlend calls them: "mutts." They don't proclaim to change the way people live or the way contractors build; in fact, they work within the realm of the standard and the familiar, elevating the off-the-shelf. Thankfully, that doesn't mean following Frank Gehry's early DIY forays or the present-day penchant for attempting to build with the waste remains of anything and everything (or mycelium!). Their impact resonates with another, broader audience that remains generally unaware of the cunning Kastler Skjeseth are carrying out with their client's Krone.

While I finished my forensic inspection of the site in Sponvika, Erlend ironed out a few more issues with Ole and then we got back in the Toyota. We stopped at a gas station for a coffee and a chocolate bar before heading back up the

Kastler Skjeseth Architects, Link House, Hølen, Norway, 2023. Photo: Max Creasy.

E6 to Oslo to collect Amandine and Erlend's two young kids, Mina and Ebba. Unexpectedly, Erlend turned east at Exit 15 and drove to what I could see, even in the twilight, was an even more picturesque spot, in Hølen. Here, we met a groovy middle-aged couple – Karen and Allan – who I'm sure had less gray hair and more cash before they hired Amandine and Erlend to link two awkwardly juxtaposed log buildings – the main house and the bryggerhus. Nothing about this was an easy assignment, and it isn't completely successful. The "link" is not Norman Foster's sleekness and lightness, and it isn't Antón García-Abril's weight and robustness. And it's definitely not Jun'ya Ishigami, whose own version of architecture's dark art often takes a more Houdini-like approach.

The two 19th-century log buildings are set about 12 meters apart and at different levels on the steep rocky site (1.2 meters) and at different angles (16 degrees). The only available space to build a link cuts across the only grass patch on the property. Externally, the link is three stepped orthogonal sections. Internally, it reads similarly, but at 1.2 meters wide – 25 square meters overall – the whole thing suffers a mild identity crisis. Is it a corridor, a habitable space, or, as Amandine and Erlend call it, a loggia? Its name, Link House, alludes to the middle choice, but at the time of my visit, Allan seemed unsure, having parked just a lone potted plant inside. The link leans to the bespoke, dare I say *bling*, side of things. It's shiny and reflective inside – I couldn't tell if it was the lights or the gloss-white paint – and it's glassy outside. I felt for the supersized soffit whose depth is a consequence of the structure's thermal mass. We only momentarily opened the custom, floor-to-ceiling glass doors to test the link's

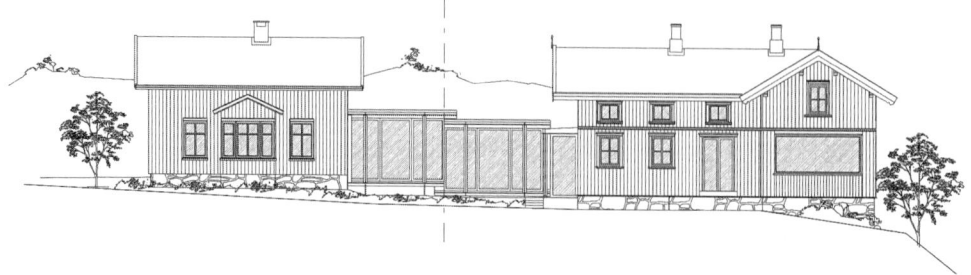

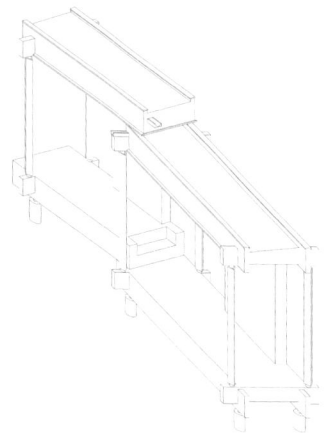

Kastler Skjeseth Architects, Link House, Hølen, Norway, 2023. Isometric. Top: Northwest elevation of the two existing buildings and the linking intervention.

loggia-likeness, which, in principle, it passed, but the darkness outside, combined with all the interior illumination, made it impossible to appreciate the floor-to-ceiling fixed-glass panels framing the rugged rock wall on the opposite side. I can almost imagine a sunny Norwegian afternoon when this stereometric affect plunges you physically and visually into the landscape, unlike anything offered by its two anchors.

The material "twist" of steel to link the two buildings is admittedly less clunky than using wood would be, but in its selection they've also succumbed to the contemporary fashion for trying to turn every local artisan into Michelangelo. The cabin in Sponvika is no less awkward, but it has more pertinent things to say about the entwined state of 21st-century society, culture, and architecture. Ultimately, the Link House does link, but it does cartwheels doing so. It was a dark winter evening when we pulled away, and as I looked back at the fully illuminated "link," there was more than a whiff of *Alpine Architektur*'s radiance in the air.

Later that night, back in Oslo, we roasted a chicken, watched *Flåklypa Grand Prix* with the kids, and talked a lot about the Norwegian economy on which the fates of Amandine, Erlend, and their handful of ambitious contemporaries lie. We discussed staying out of the grasp of "Architecture Inc.," as Erlend brands it, the cash-rich conglomerates gobbling up any and every emerging practice in their path. It was a bleak forecast. The next day, Amandine had Norwegian class and Erlend had the two kids, so Dorotea and I bundled up and headed to the third floor at Kleihues + Schuwerk's recently completed National Museum – a hulk of a building on the Oslo waterfront that would be at home in Guangzhou – to see a total mess of a show titled "Hand and Machine. Architectural drawings." It was touted as "the first exhibition of contemporary architecture at the new National Museum." Let's hope it's the last of its kind because it was as bad a show as you'll ever come across in a so-called National Museum. The only

Kastler Skjeseth Architects, Hearth House, Helgeroa, Norway, 2023. Photo: Max Creasy.

things that stuck in my mind were an elaborate glass model by LCLA and a few photos on the floor by Max Creasy (who knows why on the floor; the gallery doesn't lack for an expansive and expensive horizontal surface). Kastler Skjeseth's inclusion was limited to a tiny, badly presented drawing – actually a Lidar scan – of 19th-century painter Peder Balke's barn. Balke's barn is a well-thought-through, multiphased reuse in Østre Toten, which Kastler Skjeseth started by making a ground-to-roof scan of its scattered remnants. But at this point I was getting a long way from the log cabin, so we hurriedly escaped the museum as darkness fell again.

On our fourth and final day, a Sunday, we all went up to the office after an early pizza with the kids. Mina and Ebba watched *My Neighbor Totoro* while Amandine, Dorotea, Erlend, and I drank Japanese whiskey at an inappropriate hour and talked about the buildings I had wanted to see but couldn't. Two stood out – the log cabin in Nordmarka and the Hearth House in Helgeroa, which is another bryggerhus turned into a *hus* (aka storehouse turned into house). These two elaborate operations on existing buildings highlight the architects' ethos that heritage is an almost fictional construct.

existing section   proposed section

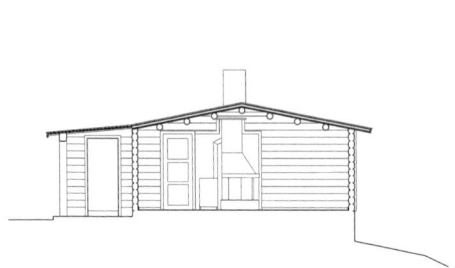
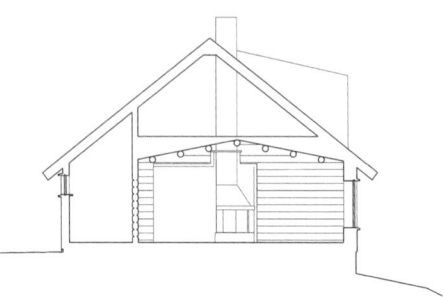

Kastler Skjeseth Architects, Log Cabin, Nordmarka, Norway, 2022. Existing and proposed east-west cross sections. Opposite page: Photos: Max Creasy.

Both projects – one consumes an existing cabin and the other removes a substantial external wall to add an extension – acknowledge the long tradition in Norwegian construction of assembling and disassembling as a form of tectonic logic. They both reject preciousness at the macroscale but are carefully considered at the microscale.

The project at Nordmarka has every ingredient you could dream of for a cabin refurbishment. Its self-minded, deep-pocketed, survivalist owner, Henrik, was seeking space and creature comfort, self-sufficiency from any state services, and a remoteness you might only associate with the cabins of the North American settler imagination. Kastler Skjeseth expanded the small and unremarkable postwar notched-log construction on a steep site to about 1.5 times its size, following the rectangular stone foundation footprint. If survivalist Bear Grylls were a building, this would be it. Surely this is architecture's real future. I love everything about it: its oddball brief; an uncompromising structural reconstruction; all the different kinds of life-sustaining "equipment" (for snow, air, solar, water, fire, gas, and soil) ornamenting its external surfaces; a click-together Plannja pitched roof with an abundant surface area that recalls the wildly underrated Norwegian Knut Knutsen's midcentury cabins and their roof-defining features, especially his Summerhouse in Portør; its out-of-scale, one-eyed Mike Wazowski–like dormer window watching over the landscape; alternating vertical and horizontal timber cladding panels acting like architectural Morse code; and its green and black exterior, which, like the bryggerhus in Lyngør, introduced me to a richer color palette than the Norwegian tourism office's globally promoted red and white.

Kastler Skjeseth cut, chopped, covered, disassembled, and filled – words rarely suggested in the "preservation" of an existing building – as necessary, and without any anthropomorphic angst, to give a whole new form

to an otherwise unchanged building type. In the process, they asked some pertinent and prescient questions about the value (or not) of a lot of contemporary architecture's more virtue-driven obsessions.

The house in Helgeroa, the conversion of an 18th-century, timber-framed storehouse, is a little more domesticated but no less utilitarian. A neat video describes the project as a simple act of slotting a new construction into a void they created on the north-facing front. Diagrammatically, it leans heavily on one of Shin Egashira's remarkable kinetic constructions in Koshirakura, Japan, the Mansuke House, which also removes an exterior surface to enter a foreign object (Erlend and Amandine both studied with Shin at the AA). In Helgeroa, the video underplays another of Kastler Skjeseth's elaborate structural reconstructions. But what really defines this project is what is becoming a bit of an obsession for them: the renovation of the building's old masonry oven. Drawing again on Venturi, Scott Brown, Amandine and Erlend have elevated almost every oven-cum-fireplace they've ever encountered to the plan's linchpin. These typically oversized, built-in masonry masses become spatial pinwheels that elaborate on another American modernist's calling card – Wright's focus on fire and food as the future.

It was almost as if the mention of another dead White man ignited Mina and Ebba's increasingly vocal protestations against the trajectory of the last waking hours of their Sunday night. That's when we called it quits, hurriedly wrapped up, and headed out into what Dorotea kept calling a "Winter Wonderland." Like the under-recognized, building-driven oeuvre of their parents, Mina and Ebba, too, had implored us to reconsider our priorities. We listened.

Christopher Pierce teaches at the AA
and has his own design studio, CaP.

Tim Altenhof

Out of the Ordinary: A Day with Peter Haimerl

Peter Haimerl wants to build 100,000 honeycomb houses. He mentions this ambition tongue in cheek as he drives his MINI Cooper Clubman toward the Bavarian Forest, home to several of his projects. Haimerl, who founded Peter Haimerl Architektur, in 1991, and is now in his early 60s, has realized a handful of idiosyncratic projects in Germany that have cemented his reputation as a nonconformist. Having arranged a day trip, we first met for breakfast at his Munich office, a small workspace above an art gallery tucked away in a residential backyard. Over coffee and berries, he said that in the early 1980s he was close to quitting his architectural studies, but then he discovered a copy of Peter Eisenman's *House X* in a bookstore in Munich, and, after reading it, he decided to continue. It resonated with the autopoetic processes and geometric modifications Haimerl was interested in at a time when the Munich scene was advocating for "smooth door handles" and "Tuscan-style brick houses." We would spend an entire day together discussing architecture and visiting several projects: a residential co-op, a small concert hall, and two revitalized farmhouses.

While still in Munich, Haimerl stops the car at the honeycomb house, the Clusterwohnen Wabenhaus, a housing cooperative based on hexagonal modules, completed in 2023. Connected by a bridge to a second, more conventional apartment building, also designed by Haimerl, the stack of honeycomb cells stands out among the uninspired rectangular boxes of the Riem district. There are no vertical interior walls except in the bathrooms and the main circulation well. The hexagons are vertically compressed so that their sides align with the slope of the central public staircase. The honeycomb house challenges the conventional dwelling and construction model in Germany, known as *Schottenbauweise*, or bulkhead construction. This system uses load-bearing walls arranged in parallel to the longitudinal axis of a residential complex. Throughout the day, we often return to the importance of language in architecture and in general. The

Peter Haimerl Architektur, Clusterwohnen Wabenhaus, Riem, Munich, 2024.
Photos: Edward Beierle.

Peter Haimerl Architektur, Clusterwohnen Wabenhaus, Riem, Munich, 2024. Cross section. All drawings courtesy the architect.

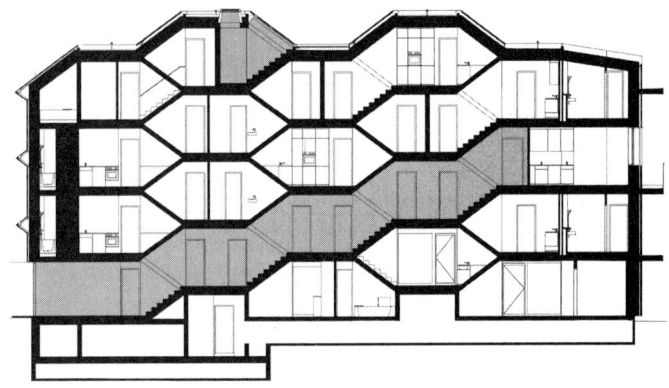

term *Schotten* resonates etymologically with *abschotten*, which means to isolate or separate. In contrast, Haimerl positions the honeycomb cells so that each is surrounded by as many as six others, promoting a closer connection among residents, despite their spatial separation. "This emotional connection is already evident," Haimerl claims. "One can feel the proximity of neighbors. The honeycomb house induces a different sense of community. Architecture, after all, is also a form of social technology." An individual hexagon may resemble a capsule, but the honeycomb house, as a whole, does not encapsulate its tenants.

We spend half an hour exploring a compact one-bedroom apartment, composed of two split-level hexagons and connected by a flight of stairs. The floor space of this unit is 31 square meters. In addition, the two hexagons each feature a three-square-meter balcony, providing two outdoor spaces at different levels. I am struck by the way this apartment challenges our cultural fixation on floor space. Despite its modest square footage, the rooms feel remarkably generous. Haimerl's introduction of the inclined wall is not new to architecture. It appears, for instance, in Moshe Safdie's unrealized 1968 project for the San Francisco State College Student Union. It also evokes Claude Parent and Paul Virilio's idea of the oblique function, which sought to bring "the body into a tactile relationship with the building."[1] In the honeycomb house, the oblique walls are fit out with custom-made furniture, cascading cushions, built-in tables, and cantilevered beds. "The typology of the inclined plane," writes Virilio, "by increasing usable surface space, also preserved that rare and extremely precious commodity: real space."[2] The interlocking, staggered cells also economize space, which is an alternative approach to addressing the scarcity of urban land for housing.

1. Pamela Johnston, ed., *The Function of the Oblique: The Architecture of Claude Parent and Paul Virilio 1963-1969*, AA Documents 3 (London: AA Publications, 1996), 5. A reference to Parent is also made in this review of the Clusterwohnen Wabenhaus: Laura Helena Wurth, "In München wurde gerade das erste Wabenhaus fertiggestellt. Bauen und Wohnen geht auch ganz anders," *NZZ*, January 11, 2024, sec. Feuilleton, https://www.nzz.ch/feuilleton/bauen-ganz-anders-das-wabenhaus-in-muenchen-ld.1771079.
2. Johnston, *The Function of the Oblique*, 13.

The first thing that comes to mind upon seeing the honeycomb is Le Corbusier's Maison Dom-Ino, as Haimerl's concept presents a new model for both dwelling and construction that can be easily replicated. While Le Corbusier proposed a system based on horizontal concrete slabs supported by columns and connected by stairs, Haimerl devised what he calls "integrated elements." The top of each hexagon is prefabricated and works structurally, spatially, and technically; it contains sound and thermal insulation as well as electrical connections and provisions for interior furnishing. Instead of concrete, a material whose controversies we would discuss later that day, a module could just as well be made of CLT (or another similar building material). Haimerl also developed a so-called cell frame, a vertical facade element enclosing the hexagons that is both structural and spatial. Additionally, prefabricated box elements form the building's core for ventilation, water supply, heating, and, potentially, elevators. While this prototype is not barrier-free – a requirement that is fulfilled by the adjacent residential building – future iterations could feature elevators that open directly onto each apartment.

Back in the car, we head toward the Bavarian Forest, where Haimerl grew up and where some of his most radical projects are located. I ask him about updating the Maison Dom-Ino diagram for the 21st century, and he says, confidently, "That is exactly what we are going to do!" While Le Corbusier established a conceptual connection between the Parthenon and the automobile, Haimerl likens his prototype to a smartphone. Like a smartphone, the house is a highly versatile yet standardized object packed with technical and aesthetic features. With a smartphone, individualization is achieved by adding a case and a personal mix of apps; in architecture, this translates to furnishing the interior. While features like built-in storage cabinets, kitchens, and triangular steps along the obliques are included in each apartment, other custom pieces must be purchased separately. This poses a challenge to the economic benefits of efficient space utilization and prefabrication. How many honeycomb houses need to be built before IKEA hops on the bandwagon? The honeycomb house is Haimerl's attempt to develop a radical new model for urban living, but affordable custom-made furniture will be crucial for the model's success.

While driving, Haimerl talks. "Twenty years ago, I decided to only do a handful of small, very special projects, for this is what architecture can actually accomplish." This decision was partly influenced by a culture in Germany that is "hostile to architecture," requiring one to "first create an environment that allows for action." It is not uncommon that Haimerl has difficulty finding German companies to realize his projects: the anti-architectural culture is matched by a lack of construction ability, exacerbated by his high expectations. For his concert hall in Blaibach, he enlisted an Austrian manufacturer from the automotive industry to produce the interior formwork. For his first renovation of a farmhouse, he sourced lightweight concrete from a Swiss firm that wasn't yet authorized in Germany. "I did almost all of my projects with manufacturing specialists from Austria," he said. This had to do with timing and cost, but also with precision, which seems at odds with the casual mentality prevalent in the Bavarian Forest, and it has left a mark on Haimerl's approach to renovating farmhouses. In vernacular Bavarian buildings, he said, one finds a casualness in craftsmanship that echoes the Japanese concept of *wabi-sabi* and its affirmation of incompleteness and imperfection.

The projects that demonstrate Haimerl's own embrace of an imperfect yet uncompromising approach are three renovated farmhouses he dubbed "houses for thinkers." Haimerl revived these dilapidated vernacular structures through an expressive use of concrete and a radical approach to repair and tradition, one that the Bavarian State Office for the Preservation of Historic Buildings – an authority one might expect to be rather reactionary – surprisingly commended as a best practice. Haimerl preserved as much of the existing farmhouses as possible while clearly distinguishing his interventions from the ruins. "There has to be a design that deals with incompleteness," Haimerl says, "that also allows strange things to collide."

And these farmhouses are strange. That day, we visited two of them. On the surface, their similarity to the honeycomb house is in the use of concrete, but their true commonality is found in Haimerl's uncompromising approach to architecture. His profound spatial understanding of habitation activates all three dimensions by virtue of split levels, nested volumes, perforated walls, and visual connections that cut through the structure. Simple and often made of wood and local granite, most of the traditional farmhouses of this area have vanished, which is partly why Haimerl wants to save the remaining ones as witnesses of a bygone era. We make a sharp left turn into the woods and drive up to a cluster of houses, one of which was his first renovation.

Dubbed Birg mich, Cilli! (Harbor me, Cilli!), Haimerl completed this project together with his wife, artist Jutta Görlich, in 2008, after a five-month halt to construction caused by his attempt to use the unapproved Swiss concrete. The contractor arrived on site to fill the formwork when local building authorities, who had "surreptitiously photographed" the construction site for several weeks, suddenly sprang into action. Only the permission of the highest federal building authorities eventually enabled completion of the project. Haimerl lined three preexisting rooms – the living room, a bathroom, and the kitchen – with concrete, transforming them into cubes with strategically placed openings that reveal the original structure. A fourth concrete cube, on the former threshing floor, creates an additional bedroom.

Upon entering, the house feels run down due to its lack of use and the rustic condition of the door. While the space recalls peasant life, its additions are too geometric and conceptual to reenact it. The austere living room, now lined with concrete, features a built-in wood board that wraps around the corner and serves as both a bench and a shelf. Evoking the typical corner benches found in farmhouses, the board is just as abstract as the square pit cut through the concrete floor that exposes the bare earth. This opening can be seen as the negative imprint of a table that no longer exists. Around the existing windows, the concrete lining pulls back to incorporate larger apertures that expose the original walls, creating a palimpsest of material layers that increases the perceived depth of the structure and of time. In its rudimentary form, this concrete layer acts as a screen that prompts introspection while allowing for external connections. It is smooth, porous, and enveloping. Three square openings in the ceiling, which can be covered by a wood hatch during winter, frame views of the existing roof structure and establish a visual connection across the entire height of the interior space.

Back in the car, we eat pretzels for lunch and discuss the house. For Haimerl, this farmhouse is a work of art that was initially conceived as a weekend retreat for his family but now stands empty. It is more a conceptual project than a preservation effort, dealing with the idea of layering and framing the preexisting structure. What makes this special, however, is the set of rooms all based on perfect squares. Initially, I thought the cubes reinforced the vernacular building, but this is not the case – the new concrete walls do not touch the existing structure. Named for its former owner, a farmwife who lived there until the 1970s, Cilli isn't just personified

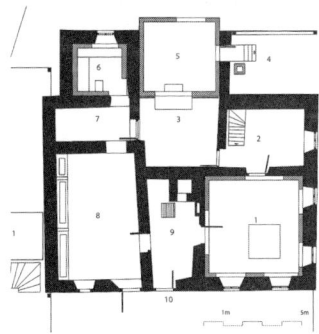

Peter Haimerl Architektur, Birg mich, Cilli!, Viechtach, Gemany, 2008. Ground floor plan with the additions shaded in gray. Top: Living room. Photo: Tim Altenhof.

by its name but also by the mentality behind the project. The new concrete cubes lack foundations, and as Haimerl explains, "I didn't want the temporal decay to freeze, but that Cilli can continue to age and also sink." In this region, cracks are an accepted feature of the structure as houses begin aging from the moment they are built and are designed to last only as long as they are inhabited. Haimerl's approach to repairing Cilli is dynamic, balancing preservation with the acceptance of aging: "I would have done violence to Cilli if I had prevented her from aging."

In Blaibach, a resort village near the Czech border, we park behind the concert hall that Haimerl completed, in 2014, as part of a coordinated effort to revitalize the village center. The building, a small concrete and granite cube, leaps out of the ground like a breaching whale. Its tilt, which follows the slope of the 200-person auditorium, is partially below grade, and its handlaid quarry stones, set by Görlich, pay homage to Blaibach's history of stone masonry. Descending the stairs into the hall, one approaches a tilted mirrored surface reflecting both the sky and the village square before turning 90 degrees toward the main entrance. Inside, a cavernous wood-paneled foyer gradually rises and falls in height as it wraps around the central concert hall, a disorienting experience that

Peter Haimerl Architektur, Konzerthaus Blaibach, Blaibach, Germany, 2014.
Photos: Tim Altenhof.

amplifies the spatial effect of the auditorium, where 3,000 foam glass panels, clad with lightweight concrete, give the feeling of being in a subterranean quarry. Where the concrete sheets drift apart, indirect lighting enhances the geological qualities of the space. In the foyer, we encounter a group of architects who have arrived for a guided tour of the concert hall, which Haimerl spontaneously decides to lead. He shares insider knowledge by explaining that the unintended pores of the lightweight concrete have little acoustical effect on the performance of the space, despite common claims about its sound-absorption properties.

The drive from Blaibach to Arnbruck, where another of Haimerl's restored vernacular structures is located, takes less than half an hour, winding through fields and woods. Denkerhaus Schedlberg, completed in 2017, is Haimerl's most iconic renovated farmhouse. To save this ruin on the brink of collapse – the house was abandoned in 1963 – Haimerl wrapped the interior with horizontal concrete beams in places where the original structure was beyond repair or entirely missing. Imagine a dentist filling cavities with a liquid material that solidifies, but where a dentist tries to make the results blend seamlessly, Haimerl's interventions are intentionally visible. Expansive glass surfaces open up the former barn and the kitchen, linking the austere interior with its bucolic surroundings. The new stacked and shifted concrete beams echo the original stacked wood beams that reinforce the gable. Haimerl also took inspiration from the moss-covered granite slabs piled up in the adjacent forest. Inside, some of these concrete beams transform into furniture, incorporating sinks or forming benches. The structure is essentially two antithetical halves that dovetail: one downhill, close to the original, cozy and dark, and one uphill, reimagined, brutalist and bright.

On the drive back to Munich, we discuss the fundamental differences between the extroverted Denkerhaus Schedlberg and the introverted Cilli. Haimerl says that the former enjoys the highest acceptance within the local community. "To the outside world, it's all bravado. People understand that. It just shows off and they have no problem with that. They only have a problem when you present something special wrapped up in a pseudo-modest white box." While the four concrete cubes in Cilli have no structural role, the concrete beams in the Denkerhaus Schedlberg actively support the old farmhouse. These two approaches to reviving vernacular buildings are profoundly distinct, yet they share a deliberate sloppiness reflected in the many surface voids in the concrete, a quality

Peter Haimerl in the kitchen of Denkerhaus Schedlberg, Arnbruck, Germany. The restoration was completed in 2017. Photos: Tim Altenhof.

that resonates with the original, aged materials, whose textures are rugged and visually rich.

As I watched the passing scenery, I thought about Haimerl's unconventional approaches to building and preservation. He pursues them with rigor and stubbornness while working in a country stifled by regulations and lackadaisical attitudes and amid growing environmental concerns about concrete as well as a dearth of experimentation in housing. For buildings to survive, they must be maintained, which can involve both technical and aesthetic modifications. Pouring concrete into existing vernacular structures not only makes effective repairs but also enhances the spatial experience. Concrete is tectonically neutral and plastic, which makes it ideal for the repair of dilapidated structures. Haimerl is not blind to the environmental drawbacks of concrete; he is simply less convinced of the benefits of timber constructions. While these vernacular houses are one-offs, the concept behind their transformations can be applied to similar buildings that have withstood the ravages of time. The Denkerhaus Schedlberg demonstrates that such structures, however ramshackle, can be elevated to spaces that honor the original while, at the same time, unlocking the potential of their reinterpretation. Such transformation endows them with a power of their own.

Imposing a new way of living, the Clusterwohnen Wabenhaus is a far cry from our ordinary idea of habitation. Given how much time most of us spend lounging, looking at our smartphones, why not engage the oblique in architecture to promote a more efficient use of space? Even if the honeycomb design fails to usher in a new dwelling paradigm, it provides a radical alternative to our entrenched living models. The architecture of Peter Haimerl can be literally inhabited: one can be inside and on top of the cubes in Cilli; the structural beams at the Denkerhaus Schedlberg form steps and benches on which to sit; the inclined planes in both the concert hall and the hexagons function as walls and infrastructure for furniture. Courage and an unwavering commitment to pursue one's ideas is what it takes to break out of the ordinary.

Tim Altenhof is a Berlin-based architect and scholar and a university assistant in architectural theory at the University of Innsbruck, where he teaches in the undergraduate program.

Observations on Three Little Houses

There once were three little houses, one of brick, one of glass, and one of paper logs. They lived happily together in their Connecticut compound, protected by a fearsome gatehouse known as Da Monsta. One hot summer day, a big bad wolf slipped past Da Monsta without a reservation. It meant business, and its business was huffing and puffing about houses. The Brick House was never worried for a minute; it knew the children's fable, and knew its very material would save it. Meanwhile, unable to shutter, the Glass House shuddered as the wolf approached. The wolf huffed and it puffed, yet was unable to blow down the Glass House's steel frame. Disaster averted. The Paper Log House watched on, more in confusion than distress. It came from a lineage of disaster-relief buildings. What was it doing here, on this idyllic New Canaan estate, where it wasn't needed? The wolf crept up, the Paper Log House gulped and braced for the worst on its milk-crate foundation.

For now, all three structures still stand awaiting friendlier visitors. But come December, by no fault of material or construction method, only the Glass and Brick houses are sure to remain. Unlike its steadfast companions, Shigeru Ban's Paper Log House is a temporary exhibit, a welcome visitor among the coterie of Philip Johnson's pavilions. Both a repeatable, hands-on lesson for the Cooper Union students who built it and a unique pavilion on the grounds of Johnson's house museum, the Paper Log House is a one-of-a-kind instance of something typically made en masse. It reminds its companions that not everyone gets to live in the comfortable climate of Connecticut. Had the big bad wolf blown it down, it could spring up someplace else, perhaps in a different form, ready to shelter victims of other big bads. – Win Overholser

Shigeru Ban, Paper Log House, New Canaan, Connecticut, April 15 – December 15, 2024. Photo: Motuma Tulu.

Motuma Tulu

Eight Days on The Butajira

"Jemo, Jemo, Jemo! Jemo, Gebriel! Jemo, Gebriel!" Taxi *redats* call out destinations as I walk out of my cousin's house in the Furi neighborhood of Addis Ababa. It's Friday morning, and the cobblestone road is bustling with three-wheeled Bajajes and pedestrians. Across the street are cafés, fruit shops, stores, and homes in mud buildings. Many of them extend to the street with an added overhead tarp. I get in the car that is waiting to take me around the city and ready my camera to document the informal architecture and economy in Addis. I start taking pictures when the cobblestone meets asphalt. Twenty or so Bajajes line both sides of the cobblestone road, and standing along the asphalt roadway are minivan taxis and their assistants – "redats" in the Amharic. We take a right and head north toward Addisu Gebeya. I immediately see the changes made in the three months I've been away.

    Addis is a rapidly evolving city due to frequent government-mandated demolitions and ensuing reconstruction by the affected communities. Modern high rises stand next to informal street vendors and horse carriages next to minivan taxis. New and old, formal and informal, wealth and poverty are often commingled. The mud houses and patchwork metal buildings in Furi quickly give way to concrete and glass structures in the Jemo and Bisrate Gebriel neighborhoods. At the border of Jemo and Bisrate Gebriel, I spot a large rectangular building with a single sloped roof angling away from the street. The striking facade, a patchwork of red painted corrugated metal, directly abuts a fence of rectangular metal sheets that step down with the slope of the street. The facade and the fence, which at first seem unified, slip past one another, revealing an unpainted patch of corrugated metal that initially registers as a slit of windows across the midsection of the building.

    Although not designed by an architect, informal buildings can be just as compelling, often achieving clever and beautiful results. But informal architecture is disappearing in Ethiopia. With globalization, the government has hopped on the "modernization" bandwagon, exchanging historical modes of building for Western ones in a bid for "progress."

Left: Bajajes line up and wait their turn to pick up riders in Arba Minch. Right: Mobile vendors line a major roadway in central Addis to peddle goods to passing cars. Beyond the jammed exit ramp, glass towers are under construction. All photos courtesy the author.

Addis Ababa, the nation's capital, is rapidly turning into a glass, steel, and concrete metropolis that can be found just about anywhere in the world, so I gravitate toward its peripheries and the interstices beyond the opulent veil of the city center and the arteries the government is actively trying to redevelop. Like the modern buildings, everyone in them looks eerily similar, as the informal workers have been relegated to the corners of the city, where land ownership is still ambiguous.

The vernacular is found where people construct their own dwellings, businesses, and communities, keeping Ethiopia's craft-based traditions alive. These structures don't have the clean and polished look of what the government terms modern because they are often jerry-rigged in the loose and permissive way that working-class people construct their buildings and configure their communities. I'm fond of the patchworked metal and tarp, bamboo, mud, raw wood, and stone constructions. This architecture creates spaces for community gathering and informal work, which are intrinsic to Ethiopia's way of life. So, for the third time in a year, I've come to document the jerry-rigged constructions that are slowly disappearing along the Butajira [bü-'ta-ji-ra] roadway, making an 800-kilometer journey from Addis Ababa, in central Ethiopia, to Turmi, near the southwest border with Kenya. The route passes through a region of Ethiopia that is as architecturally diverse as it is ethnically.

Shaggar
After spending the day documenting various jerry-rigged constructions in Addis, I head to my brother's gray concrete house on the northwest side of the city. He lives next to

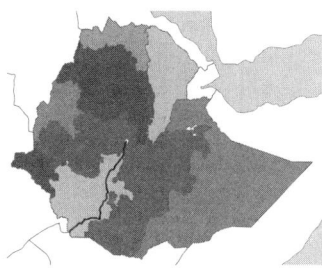

Ethiopia is divided into 13 regions and 68 zones. The stops along the 800-kilometer trip on the Butajira, from Addis to Turmi, are marked according to population size.

Mount Entoto, an area surrounded by towering blue-green eucalypti that color the landscape and fill the air with their fragrant scent. At sunrise on Saturday, I slip into his manual Toyota Prado and plunge into Addis's morning traffic, heading southwest to Shaggar City. Shaggar is the result of a government plan to group periphery neighborhoods and districts around Addis to establish a zone for a future smart city. To do so, the government has enforced long-ignored zoning codes, causing hundreds of thousands of buildings to be razed in just the past few years. At the moment, Shaggar is a mix of informal settlements, new upscale housing developments, and small businesses in ubiquitous three-by-three-meter structures. These dimensions originate from the three-meter length of corrugated metal sheets, and over time, the dimension has become typical of many businesses, regardless of the building material.

At the *adebabay*, or roundabout, where Shaggar begins, there are horse carriages, Bajajes, motorcycles, and a number of patchwork corrugated metal structures. Souks expand

A watchtower sits atop a crude wood structure overlooking a neighborhood at the edge of Shaggar.

their operations onto the sidewalks and mobile businesses spill into the streets. The roadway, sidewalk, and building zone blur as pedestrians move seamlessly from one to the other. The street is no longer vehicle only. When cattle appear I slow down, and the car joins the melange of the extravehicular crowd.

At the edge of Shaggar, I pass a watchtower sticking up between sheets of corrugated metal like a head poking above a fence. The quirky little box, just large enough for one person, sits atop a crude wood platform, its eccentric form reminiscent of the fairy tale–esque tea houses of Japanese architect Terunobu Fujimori. Wires run down from it, suggesting the presence of an electric light, maybe even an outlet. The tower is an example of consolidating resources and taking up the least amount of space, while accommodating a guard who keeps watch over a family or neighborhood at night.

Oromo Region and Gurage Zone

Ethiopia is subdivided into large regions and localized zones based on its more than 80 ethnic groups, most with their own languages and cultures. After Addis, a neutral zone that doesn't fall under the jurisdiction of any one ethnic group, I arrive in the Oromo Region. Near the entry to the town of Bu-i are furniture-fabrication workshops that use small mud and patchwork metal buildings for storage and larger corrugated metal and tarp structures to work in or under. In the Gurage Zone that follows, the cities are larger but farther apart. Between them are many *sar bets*, or grass-roofed huts, their round mud walls topped by conical thatched roofs and painted with figures in many colors. In the town of Butajira are several game houses, where young men gather to play pool or table tennis. Much like the workshops in Bu-i, game houses occupy structures framed with crude wood and covered with tarps or corrugated metal sheets, which are perhaps the most versatile materials due to their modularity, availability, and affordability.

Hosaena

Leaving the town of Butajira, I drive 100 kilometers to my hometown of Hosaena, in the Hadiya Zone. I arrive around noon, drop off my bags at my uncle's house, and take a Bajaj with my aunt to the *gebeya*, or market, near the town center. Better than a car, the small Bajaj can more easily navigate the streets clogged with vehicles, animals, and pedestrians on gebeya day. Every Saturday farmers and merchants set

In the city of Hosaena, concrete towers are interspersed with mud houses with corrugated metal roofs. The Hosaena market sets up every Saturday in the field at the top right.

up goods at their designated stalls by stretching multicolored tarps over wood structures. The overlapping tarps form a colorful, shifting landscape above the gradually sloping market grounds. Shoppers carry baskets called *zembils*, donkeys pull carts, and wheelbarrow drivers push heavy loads. On the streets leading to the market, mobile vendors take advantage of the foot traffic, lining the streets to compete with local businesses. In the market, salesmen call out products and prices like mantras as I walk down row upon row of stalls, bargaining, and occasionally feigning disinterest to get a better price. Stalls offering similar products are grouped together. At the vegetable stalls, sunlight filters through the tarps, bathing the people and produce in blue and orange hues. The pungent scents of herbs and spices waft through the air, drawing me to bright red, green, and yellow mounds of *mitmita*, *berbere*, *ihrd*, and *korerima*, packed high. In the crafts area, *agelgils* (woven containers for food), *gandas* (round clay containers for liquid), *jebenas* (clay coffee pots), and other cultural staples line the stalls. The taller textile stalls display hanging curtains, mats, and *gabis* (cotton blankets with patterned ends). Then, at sunset, as if a spell has been broken, the cacophony of bargaining, the merchandise, the scents, and the colors rapidly drain from the market. All that remains is a field of spindly wood structures, skeletons of otherworldly beasts waiting to be reanimated.

A mechanic works in a three-by-three-meter container. Stacked wheels and tires are the sign of an auto repair shop.

Early Sunday, I start driving around Hosaena, taking stock of the changes since my last visit. What was a small town when I was a child has, over the past 15 years, become a stereotypical bustling city in Ethiopia. Wealthy individuals are increasingly trying to develop the roadside frontage, but the compounds along the roadway have historically been owned by people of modest means, whose buildings are mostly mud constructions with a front veneer that gives the illusion of metal construction. Businesses occupy the minimum space required for their needs while achieving a high degree of functionality. The three-by-three-meter souks are not seen as limiting boundaries; their frontage is often used for display and selling. At the north end of town, construction-related businesses sell lumber, untreated wood, steel beams and sheets, stone, and other building materials in open yards. Down the street, hardware stores and workshops display furniture and prefabricated building materials from corrugated metal structures or under tarps that extend from three-by-three-meter mud houses. Nearby, auto mechanics mostly operate out of three-by-three-meter corrugated metal buildings with spaces out front for working on one or two cars. In the town center are mini malls, banks, and office buildings, and to the south is the *menaria*, where buses and minibuses line up. Since most people don't own cars, they travel between cities by bus or minibus. Around the menaria, which is the busiest part of town, mobile vendors peddle clothing, food, and household supplies from wagons. Other mobile businesses such as *listros*, who clean shoes, occupy leftover pockets of space near local businesses or in abandoned or halted construction sites. A number of structures are scaled up forms of craftwork such as weaving, including woven wood fences that incorporate growing vegetation. At cafés throughout the town, people sit on porches or under the shade of a tree and drink coffee together.

Like most Ethiopian cities, the "center" of Hosaena is not concentric but linear, running along the two roadways that enter the city from the northwest and the northeast and coalesce into a single roadway at the adebabay before heading south toward the city of Sodo. Cities in Ethiopia began to develop in a linear manner after the Italian occupation, from 1936 to 1941. Italy failed to colonize Ethiopia in the 19th century, so they invaded again in 1935, successfully capturing Addis in 1936, but they were still unable to occupy the entire country due to local resistance. The Italians quickly built highways to connect the cities they had captured, but

A mud building and a stick building, both with porches and corrugated metal roofs, along the roadway. The exposed trusses in the stick building are made from eucalyptus trunks supported by eucalyptus poles threaded together with horizontal eucalyptus branches. Beneath its exterior, the mud building has a similar wood structure.

the Ethiopian resistance, with British military aid, forced the Italians out of the country in 1941. Ethiopia then entered an era of rapid modernization, rebuilding cities and continuing highway construction. As existing towns grew and new ones developed, people built along the highways that connected them. But when the highways became the city centers, they stopped being speedy thoroughfares. Pedestrians, cattle, mobile vendors, and mini-vehicles occupied the thoroughfares, congesting them, which in turn reinforced the roadways as city centers. Today, both fixed and mobile businesses peddle their goods to those with cars, who tend to be wealthier, and to those traveling between cities.

Doyogena

After driving around Hosaena for an hour, I head south toward Sodo. The road is pocked with potholes after years without proper maintenance. I weave between ruts and dodge pedestrians and cattle as the road twists and turns up and down the highlands, and drivers accommodate one another to safely navigate the difficult terrain.

Entering the Kembata Zone, I slowly pass through Doyogena, a town composed mostly of mud houses with corrugated metal roofs. There's no metal veneer like in Hosaena. A mud wall is constructed by vertically stacking stripped eucalyptus trunks and bracing them horizontally with eucalyptus branches, then plastering mud mixed with chaff to the wood. The houses are often built by their owners with the

Top: Three bays on the first floor of a concrete structure that is under construction are rented to shops in order to generate income to finish the building. Below: Outside a row of modular storage rooms, salesmen spill sacks of grain onto tarps so shoppers can buy by the measure.

help of the community. My childhood home in Hosaena was also made with mud, and like the typical mud house, it had a porch supported by thin metal columns. Most buildings in Doyogena have porches, but they're generally supported by thin wood poles. Porches are an affordable way to extend a business or home and also take advantage of the temperate highland climate. By drawing on a domestic typology, a souk with a porch can add a café where people can gather to eat and drink.

Sodo

I arrive in Sodo, in the Wolaita Zone, at 10:00 am. The road bends sharply at the town entry then leads to the market streets. Ahead, an Isuzu truck unloading sacks of grain is creating a minor traffic jam. While my car is stuck behind it, Bajajes and motorcycles maneuver past me and the truck like a murmuration of starlings. In central Addis, passenger transport by Bajaj and motorcycle is banned, so people are forced to take minivan taxis. These have increased in number in accordance with the growing population, leading to heavy congestion during rush hour and on rainy days. This isn't a problem in the peripheries of Addis or in Sodo, where Bajaj and motorcycle transportation is allowed.

As I slowly begin to follow the now-empty truck, grain salesmen are already peddling their products. Most of them operate from a row of modular rooms in long rectangular buildings, where the grain is stored. The grain is brought out to the sidewalk, a few bags at a time, and spilled onto large tarps so people can purchase it by the kilo. Other grain salesmen operate from a row of three-by-three-meter corrugated

A café operates from under a makeshift porch in a concrete building that has been sawed back to the setback line, perhaps to comply with zoning laws.

metal structures that extend to the sidewalk with jerry-rigged tarp canopies.

Turning left, I find rows of small concrete souks, their goods also spilled out along the street for display. Among them is an unfinished two-story concrete structure, with a souk, or perhaps multiple souks, tucked in the three bays of the first floor. Rows of freestanding columns hold up the two exposed slabs, and threads of rebar crown the top of the upper slab, anticipating future construction. Corrugated metal is used as a makeshift ceiling on the first floor, and a white textile stretched between the second-floor slab and a gate outside the building marks inhabited spaces. The structure, like many throughout Ethiopia, is a sign of the difficulty in getting construction loans. It is common to build large structures incrementally, with habitable spaces in unfinished buildings rented out to collect funds to finish the construction. In the meantime, such buildings exist in a jerry-rigged state as the inhabitants appropriate spaces to meet their needs.

Arba Minch

After photographing buildings in Sodo, I drive 120 kilometers south to the city of Arba Minch, in the Omo valley, arriving in the early evening. Unlike most of Ethiopia, which is highlands, the Omo valley is a hot region. Its many unique tribes continue to lead nomadic and pastoral lifestyles. I head toward the center of Arba Minch, rounding many adebabays along the way. Close to the town center I spot a two-story concrete building that has clearly been sawed through, its jagged ends like open wounds. In a state of partial ruin – whether by natural causes or government-mandated demolition – such buildings

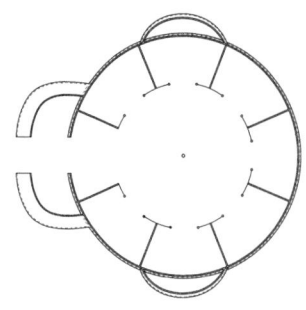

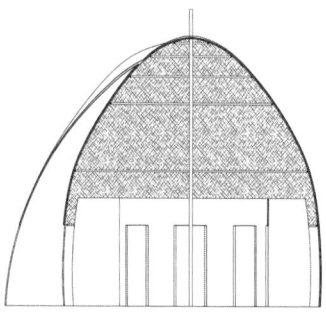

Top: Plan of a Dorze gojo; bedrooms and storage are set along the perimeter, and the central room is a communal space for cooking and lounging. Below: Section of a Dorze gojo; the woven bamboo room partitions rise just halfway up the space. Drawings courtesy the author.

are often maintained by their owners, who give them a second life. Buildings that would generally be abandoned or torn down in the West are rehabilitated in Ethiopia, often through unconventional means. In this one, which reminds me of Le Corbusier's Maison Dom-Ino, wood poles at the edges of the slabs support both floors. On the first floor are a barbershop and a café, where people sit outside on plastic stools, eating, drinking coffee, and chatting. Given the setback of the street front, the cuts seem to be another instance of local officials deciding to enforce previously ignored zoning codes. Rebar sticks up from the ground, marking where a concrete column was removed. Unlike the typical result of government-mandated teardowns, this rehabilitated ruin might be an improvement. Concrete buildings are a sign of wealth, but in its current state, this building blends in with the streetscape because it now resembles the mud houses with thin eucalyptus poles supporting porch roofs.

Arba Minch is a resort town. Here, most hotels are called resorts. I head to one where I have previously stayed and check in, dropping off my bags in a modern approximation of a sar bet – a gimmick for foreigners – and head to dinner at Paradise Resort. It has some of the best food in town. I order their fish soup, which tastes like *key whet* – a spicy traditional stew – and a fruit salad; the hot climate produces some of the best fruits I've ever eaten. The fish is freshly caught from Chamo, a lake visible in the distance from this cliff-top resort.

Dorze Village

On Monday morning, I drive just 20 minutes before turning left onto an asphalt road that rapidly turns to gravel. I slowly steer the Prado up the steep inclines to Dorze Village. As the gravel turns to dirt, woven bamboo fences begin to appear around false banana groves. Amid the false banana trees, called *enset*, are unique sar bets, clad with rounded enset leaves called *coba*. Since *sar bet* translates to grass-roofed hut, the term *gojo bet*, or *gojo*, meaning hut, is more accurate because Dorze gojos are clad in coba. Enset is the lifeblood of the Dorze and most southern Ethiopia tribes. While the coba is used for cladding, the stem of the enset is used to make a dough called *bulla*, which can be made into a bread called *kocho* and a jello-like food called *genfo*. The fibers of the stem are also woven into mats, baskets, and ropes. My maternal grandparents, who were farmers in Wesheba, a rural village near Hosaena, also grew enset. When our extended family would gather at their home for holidays, many of us would

Top: A Dorze tribe gojo, which resembles an elephant, is bounded by a woven bamboo fence and ensets. Below left: A woven bamboo bench is under a woven bamboo covering. Right: Outside of a Dorze gojo, a man sits on a stone to weave a textile on a bamboo loom.

The woven bamboo roof structure of a Dorze gojo is anchored by a single wood pole.

sleep on *jibas*, soft mats woven from the fibers of enset stems. My last memory of my grandfather is of seeing him sitting at the doorway of a sar bet, weaving enset threads into rope for tethering the cows. As a curious 12-year-old, I asked to help, and he humored me by giving me some threads. When I finished, he studied the thin, tangled weave and, grinning, cheekily said, "Well, this will be good for tying chickens."

I arrive at the tourism post to hire one of the tribe's guides – a local requirement – and then head into the village. The Dorze are a close-knit community; their households are interlinked with woven bamboo fences that also establish the boundaries of each dwelling. The gojos resemble elephants – ears, eyes, and trunk included – a product of the Dorze's historically close relationship with elephants before the elephant population declined and then disappeared from the area.

The Dorze are masters of bamboo. When people marry, they build themselves a house, using bamboo for their home, for fences, and almost all furniture. The interior resembles a giant basket that starts with thick strips of mature bamboo, which is strong but less pliable, woven into loose patterns at the base, with gradually decreasing strip sizes in tighter weaves as the structure is built up. The more malleable unripe bamboo is used to make nonstructural elements. A tall, thin pole in the middle of the sar bet supports the center of the roof. To repair

Section of a Konso community sar bet. Right: A Konso community sar bet sits on a stacked stone base and is surrounded by stacked stone walls that frame a courtyard for gatherings.

or maintain a gojo, the coba cladding and the woven bamboo can be taken apart and new material woven in. Gojos can even be picked up and relocated as necessary.

The Dorze's mastery of weaving extends to textiles as well. From a young age, both boys and girls are taught to weave; the women spin cotton into threads that the men use to weave textiles. The Dorze's use of bamboo, enset, and cotton embodies an ecologically balanced lifestyle that extends to planting, harvesting, and eating sustainably, a practice that is becoming increasingly foreign in modernizing Ethiopia.

A Konso Village

After spending most of the day in Dorze Village, I head back down the mountain, returning to Arba Minch for the night. The next morning, I hit the road for the town of Karat, which is 90 kilometers away. Most of the road is gravel and there are few towns along it, likely due to the semidesert condition. In Karat, I hire a local from the tour guide office to accompany me to a Konso village, since I don't speak their language. Around noon, we turn off an asphalt road onto a red dirt road, drive five minutes, and park at the edge of the village. It's a sweltering 90 degrees Fahrenheit, and the sun is beating down as the guide slowly leads me through meandering streets framed by stacked stone walls. The red earth dusts everything with a coppery hue. I take pictures as the guide explains the history and building techniques of the village. The heat quickly becomes unbearable. When we arrive at the center of the village, I practically run to sit under the shade of a large sar bet surrounded by tall, stacked stone walls. Instantly, it feels 20 degrees cooler. Sar bets are designed to funnel heat up and out through the thatched roof, keeping those sitting under it cool.

This sar bet is a communal gathering space, with large aged-wood poles supporting the log floor of a second level. A central pole extends from a stacked stone base and through a rectangular opening in the log floor to support the thatched roof. Some people sit on the stone base, others sit on stone benches that extend from the surrounding stone walls. Elderly men play a game with white pebbles on a wood board that I'm not familiar with, while elderly women spin cotton and children run about. There are almost no young or middle-aged adults around because they are working in the fields or in their homes. During the day, community members gather on the first level. At night, married men who have newborn children at home sleep on beds of animal hides on the second level, according to the tribe's tradition.

Finally feeling cool enough to enjoy the sar bet's design and the towering copper-toned stone walls framing a courtyard around it, I take pictures, occasionally lying down to get a better angle of the underside of the woven stick roof, which reminds me of the Dorze tribe's gojos. Children gather around me, putting their hands under my head to keep my hair clean, dusting me off, and trying to look at the pictures I take. Seeing their curiosity, I hand them the camera by turn and show them how to photograph what interests them. More villagers gather around, and the sar bet becomes lively with conversation and activity. The women show me their intricate weaving techniques and their finished textiles, some of which I buy. After about 45 minutes, having completely cooled off, I leave the sar bet and make my way to a church that was being erected when I visited three months ago.

Now nearly finished, the church is a beautiful wood structure with the reddish tone of the earth. The wall is made of varying eucalyptus trunks stacked vertically and threaded together horizontally with long branches. Inside, the daylight filters through the variable arrangements of sticks, casting shadows that dance across the floor and creating an ethereal experience under the makeshift wood trusses that hold up the corrugated metal roof. I am reminded of the housing for healthcare workers in Rwanda, designed by New York architect Sharon Davis, where thin sticks form a screen that creates an interstitial space, dappled with light during the day and at night acts like a lantern. Pritzker Prize laureate Francis Kéré also uses arrangements of crude wood to create beautiful screens. For the Lycée Schorge, in Burkina Faso, Kéré leans long thin poles of wood at different angles to create a screen offset from the facade, similar to Davis, that reads like

The construction of the stick-built church at the edge of the Konso village frames a cross on one end. Light filters through the facade into the interior, where rows of wood poles support makeshift trusses that hold up the corrugated metal roof.

an undulating sheet. These are not unique examples, but a seeming trend for many architects working in Africa, including Shigeru Ban, who, in 2017, designed a shelter from tree branches in northern Kenya, extending the lineage of his Paper Log House. These "modern" buildings derive from stick constructions that can be found throughout Ethiopia and sub-Saharan Africa.

Hamar Tribe

After two hours in the Konso village, I drive 150 kilometers in 100 plus degree heat without AC to Jinka, where I spend the night at a hotel tucked amid a small forest. On Tuesday morning, I visit the Benna tribe, near the town of Key Afer, which means red dirt, before heading 80 kilometers south to Turmi, in the South Omo Zone. My last stop is at one of the Hamar tribe's villages, five minutes north of Turmi. The tribe's huts sprawl across the copper-red landscape. As I park the car, the nearly setting sun casts an incandescent glow that filters through the woven stick fences separating the households and defining the pathways between them. The red sun, red earth, and red dust coat everything, creating a surreal landscape, almost like being in an impressionist painting. As villagers come to welcome me, their appearance only heightens the painted quality. Their bare, sun-bronzed torsos, adorned with multicolored beads, have a metallic sheen that's accented by the shimmering dust on their skin. Hamar households dwell together in circular sar bets made of thin stick walls capped by thatched roofs. The sar bets look small from the outside but their interiors are, as if by magic, expansive.

A young Hamar man adorned with beads stands in front of a woven stick fence.

These sar bets remind me of my grandparents' sar bet in Wesheba. Theirs was bounded by a circular mud wall and capped by a conical thatched roof. From the outside, the hut seemed no larger than the span of my arms but it seemed to grow 10 times in size when I entered through its wood door. Like most huts, a monumental wood pole at the center anchored the radiating wood members that held up the thatched roof. The sar bet was actually the cattle house. The animals stayed to the right side of the door; chickens, sheep, cows, and horses. People, the more than 20 members of our family, sat to the left. At dusk, people would trickle in, some taking their usual places on makeshift seating, others sitting on the dirt floor. We would gather around coal fires and lanterns – there was no electricity – laughter brightening the dim expanse. Cows quietly chewed cud, sheep occasionally bleated, and the chickens softly clucked.

The stick walls of a Hamar tribe sar bet are similar to the woven stick fence that defines the bounds of the community.

We would eat simple meals, mostly vegetables. My favorite was my grandmother's *ayib*, a cheese and herbal butter dish served cold with kocho. The main house, a mud house next to the sar bet, was no more than a sleeping barrack. The sar bet was where we chose to gather, its almost magical quality drawing us in.

Doro-Manekia

After a night in Turmi, I turn the car around to begin the 800-kilometer drive back to Addis. Over the course of two days, I stop again in Arba Minch and then in Hosaena to spend the night and to see family. On the third day, upon returning to Addis, I return the car to my brother. The next day, he and I head to the butcher shop street in Doro-Manekia, a sub-neighborhood of Piassa in the center of Addis. We take a right off Piassa Boulevard onto a narrow cobblestone street and drive up to our usual *migib bet*, or restaurant, where an informal parking attendant helps my brother perform the acrobatics required to park on the tight street. Parking attendants like this one also watch over the cars for a small tip, usually 10 birrs (20 cents USD). We walk up to a butcher shop window, where a butcher stands in front of large sides of meat hanging in a red and white painted room, colors that indicate a butcher. We ask for our usual half kilo of beef to be sent to the kitchen for what I believe is the best *tibs* in town: cubes of

The Toyota Prado navigates a cobblestone street in Doro Manekia, where informal parking attendants help drivers find just enough room to park.

beef pan seared with *kibe* – an herb-infused butter – spices, and substantial amounts of fat to give it a crust. We dip under a wood doorframe and find seats in the blue-painted mud house, joining 15 or so people in a room with a seating capacity of 10. As the server comes to take our drink order, he calls me *abaye* (the common term of endearment for a guy). When their food comes, the people next to us say *enibla* (eat with us).

From the parking attendant to the butcher, the mud house, the server, and the migib bet, the neighborhood of Doro Manekia is representative of a lifestyle intrinsic to Ethiopia in both urban and rural communities. The modern buildings in central Addis foster a new type of social life that is Western oriented and caters to the wealthy. However, most Ethiopians are of modest means and reliant on the informal economy and culture of gathering that are part and parcel of informal building practices. Driving down the Butajira, it was clear that informal structures give working-class people greater ability to build their own homes and businesses and places for communities to gather, thereby achieving a self-sustaining way of life. And while the government might seek to erase these structures, labeling them ramshackle, the often crude and eccentric forms have a unique appeal, even though their emphasis is on efficiency, not an aesthetic.

In a time fraught with crisis fatigue – economic, political, and environmental – it's easy to overlook what might, at first glance, appear too simple or crude to be considered architecture. Perhaps the nimble building techniques in Ethiopian cities can teach us how to accept looser and more permissive practices that could provide alternate modes of habitation and economy and add to our repertoire of sustainable practices. And along the way, we may even inherit a new appreciation for an aesthetic of making do.

Motuma Tulu recently graduated with a master of architecture from Princeton. A special thanks to Fantahun Tulu, Abreham Abera, Balemi Habtamu, and Dawit Alemu for all of your help in making this journey possible.

Observations on Homegrown

This summer, sprawling installations at the New York Botanical Garden in the Bronx take visitors into a fantastical land of curiosities and wild impossibilities. Curated by art historian Jennifer Gross, "Wonderland: Curious Nature" was inspired by Lewis Carroll's Alice's Adventures in Wonderland, the 1865 novel published at a time when naturalists were dramatically reshaping the understanding of the world.

To draw on the story's play with mushrooms, Gross commissioned London-based architect Andre Kong to design Homegrown, a cottage using mycelium. Kong collaborated with the biomaterials company Ecovative to grow mycelium blocks. Using hemp substrate purchased from local farmers, Ecovative sterilized and stored the material before inoculating it with fungi to create a self-assembling "mushroom material." After three to four days of mycelium growth, the material is broken up and sealed in rectangular thermoform molds to form a solid mass. When popped out of the molds, the blocks are baked at 100–150 degrees Fahrenheit to remove moisture, stop growth, and harden.

Kong's mycelium work stems from his proposal for the 2023 London Festival of Architecture's EcoHome Pavilion Competition for innovative domestic solutions to the climate crisis. His team identified thermal performance as the UK's biggest challenge in existing housing and proposed growing biodegradable net carbon zero

andre kong studio, Homegrown, "Wonderland: Curious Nature," May 18 – October 27, 2024, New York Botanical Garden. Photo courtesy the architect and NYBG.

insulation from scratch, thereby producing an alternative for insulating aging homes.

The Homegrown cottage suggests that mycelium blocks could also be used as an expressive architectural element, not just hidden behind plasterboard. The blocks act as infill that "grows out" to windows and doors set in a timber frame, giving the roof and walls an organic sculptural form.

Looking through the gaps between the mycelium blocks, one can see the landscape from which, like a mushroom, Homegrown seems to have sprung.

– Riley Grills

Observations on Digital Drawing

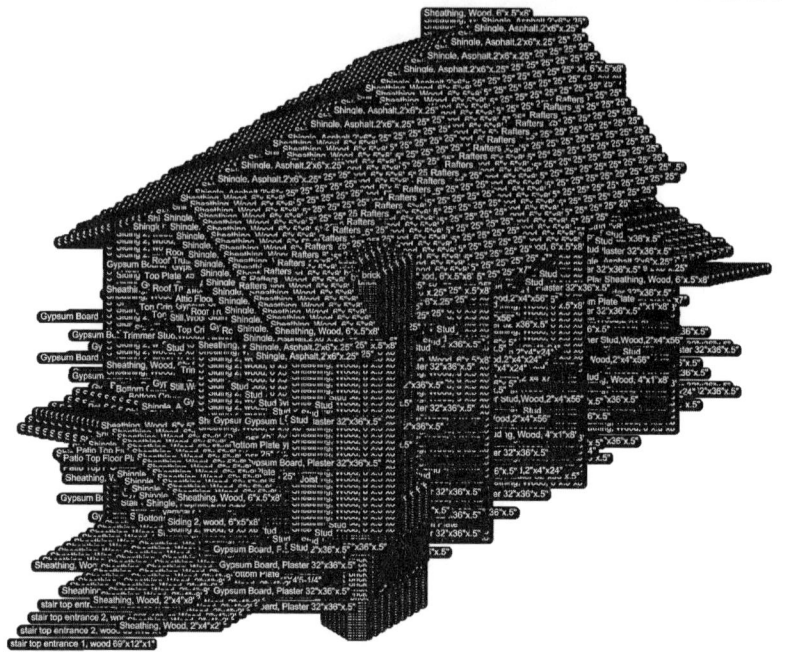

As artificial intelligence and large language models continue to evolve, the ability to represent architecture through language and text will become crucial. Generative models will disrupt drawing-based architectural representation, shifting the production of architecture from descriptive geometry to text-based data. Nero Chenxuan He's image, created for a Texas Tech University studio, represents a shift toward using data as architectural representation. The drawing gives new agency to the process of documenting and tagging by challenging traditional visual standards and presenting architecture as pure text.

Instead of curve, surface, or solid modeling, the studio documents various Sears kit houses as a series of material assembly text annotations. Every architectural element, from door hinges to roof shingles, appears as a text annotation. Students then designed their projects solely through text annotations, sampling, curating, and recombining. The image, with its absence of typical geometric elements and focus on text, mirrors the low-level computer-information processing that is fundamental to large language models.

The proposed replacement of drafting with data provokes interesting questions. Should architects be as adept with table queries as we are with drawing perspectives? Can we master data as we mastered descriptive geometry? This may require deromanticizing notions of what constitutes the architecture profession, as it relates to drawing, and reconsidering pedagogical approaches. Drawing descriptive geometry (sometimes still by hand) is prioritized in architectural education, while computational courses are often offered only as advanced electives. Amid the AI revolution, where will data and coding literacy fit in the curriculum? The dominance of text representation seems imminent. How will architects maintain design agency as the practice evolves from the straightedge to the spreadsheet?

— Matt Conway

Nero Chenxuan He, Text Dot 3D Material Documentation, 2024, reimagines architectural representation through text annotations, depicting the Sears catalog "Honor Bilt" Norwood prefabricated kit house with each element tagged.

Ben Fehrman-Lee

Vision in the Hands Of the Visionary

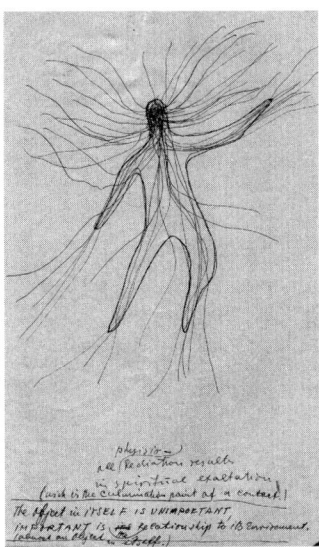

Frederick Kiesler, All physical radiation (...), 1938–41. Ink on paper, 21 by 14 centimeters. © Austrian Frederick and Lillian Kiesler Private Foundation, Vienna. Presented in "Frederick Kiesler: Vision Machines," April 25 – July 28, 2024, Jewish Museum, New York. All images courtesy the Jewish Museum.

Responsive. Flexible. Adaptive. Mobile. Organic. One could just as easily be describing contemporary design principles as the ambitions, research, and preoccupations of the famed early 20th-century multidisciplinary designer and architect Frederick Kiesler. The brief but immersive exhibition "Frederick Kiesler: Vision Machines," recently on view at the Jewish Museum in New York, brought Kiesler's transdisciplinary design practice into focus during the years he directed the Laboratory for Design Correlation at Columbia University, from the late 1930s into the 1940s, and its two most important outcomes: the Mobile Home Library and the Vision Machine.

Curated by Mark Wasiuta, codirector of the Critical, Curatorial & Conceptual Practices in Architecture program at Columbia, the exhibition also traced Kiesler's obsession with sight, looking, reading, and dreams – visualizing the phenomenon of vision. Among several dozen typewritten notes in the exhibition, one with Kiesler's brief description of the concept of the Vision Machine, from 1938, stood out: "Through this demonstration we learn that neither light, nor eye, nor brain, alone or in association, can see. But rather, we see only through the total coordination of human experiences; and even then, it is our own conceived image, and not really the actual object which we perceive. We learn, therefore, that we see by creative ability and not by technical reproduction." He employs terminology like "eye-beam" and "eye-brain," in handwritten notes, to articulate projection and reception of light in three-dimensional space. He reflects on how both the eye and the subconscious mediate objects and images. He formulates everything around the "biotechnique," or the total physiology of the human and the extension of sight through them. He deals so heavily in abstraction that he bends toward the surreal. And in this show, almost all of it was presented through his drawings, collages, and diagrams.

On more than a few occasions, Kiesler's work and imaginations have been praised as "prescient," his ideas preceding responsive design and environments, interfaces, networked archives, and information systems all by some 20, 30, and even 60 years. But equally prescient to these modal outcomes

Frederick Kiesler, Mobile Home Library, fabricated for the exhibition in 2024. Photo: Kris Graves. Opposite page: Frederick Kiesler, Mobile Home Library as represented in the "Manifesto of Correalism," 1947. © Austrian Frederick and Lillian Kiesler Private Foundation, Vienna.

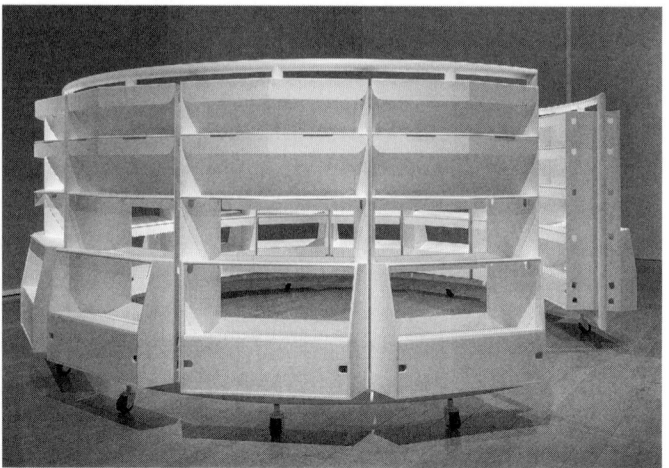

is Kiesler's transdisciplinary approach to architectural and industrial design: his ultimate theory of correalism, as codified in the "Manifesto of Correalism," claims that everything relates or connects to everything.

Kiesler was born in 1890, in an area of Austria-Hungary now known as Ukraine, and moved to New York in 1926. A small prologue to the exhibition featured some of Kiesler's earliest commissions in New York, including a constructivist-inspired moving cylindrical stage design for Julliard School performances, and a responsive, adaptive cinema screen that could modify its size and dimension for the medium of film. In these, he sought to activate a conventionally static context, and these few samples possessed early notions of his matured theories of correlation.

If we take Kiesler's premise of correalism seriously, then we can all the more appreciate Wasiuta's curatorial direction, which put speculative drawings and typewritten notes in conversation with things we might associate more formally with "architecture" and did not distinguish between them. Too often a curatorial hierarchy separates major formulations from minor ideas. Here, Kiesler's ideas were side by side, without such differentiation. Architecture became a medium for performance or for living, an interface for viewers, and a browsing system for users. The speculations and preoccupations of Kiesler's broader interests obviously informed the more pragmatic details of building for specific commissions, and vice versa. In his own terms, every one of his undertakings connects to everything else, each coloring the other.

The exhibition, on the upper floor of the museum, was focused and immediate, which was to the viewer's advantage because these artifacts took time to digest. The first room

was devoted to the Mobile Home Library, which, for the first time, was constructed in its entirety at scale. The second room focused on the Laboratory of Design Correlation at Columbia, and the last room was an expansive survey of Exhibition Machines, or apparatuses for arranging, looking at, and experiencing artworks.

One of the significant outcomes of the Laboratory of Design Correlation was the Mobile Home Library, a circular shelving system composed of 11 dual-sided vertical bays of shelves, each unit rotating independently on a central axis, arranged in a circular frame that surrounds the browser. It is the result of a prompt to redesign something that is an established and functional design: a bookshelf. Kiesler's concept for the library is reminiscent of the planetary revolutions of the solar system; in a way, it places the browser at the orbital center of information – books, in this case. Wasiuta and his team painstakingly fabricated the library to Kiesler's exact specifications, only updating its material. In nearby photographs of original prototypes, viewers could see the original material specs, such as sheet metal or wood, and appreciate the evolution. The material substitution of white powder-coated steel also gave Wasiuta's fabrication a new sense of aura, a ghost of the past made manifest for a contemporary context.

A rotating viewing machine based on a Kiesler sketch for a new mechanism to display multiple items at once. Photo: Kris Graves.

There is a stark contrast between Kiesler's outsized imagination and the context in which he sought to apply it. His drawings, doodles, and diagrams sometimes border on the fantastical, but most of his preoccupations seem to be very human, even domestic, in scale. The documents collected in the second room, featuring work done in the Laboratory of Design Correlation, reflect the devotion of Keisler and his students to human physiology. A clever, automated, rotating set of vitrines allowed the viewer to see these pieces in motion, rather than in static contexts. A keen eye might have spotted a preliminary sketch of this very structure among the other artifacts. While each item was numbered for reference, there was no beginning, middle, or end to this material but rather a looping continuum of ideas, drawings, prototypes, and studies – a kind of analog browsing window or endless scroll for the viewer.

The third and largest room presented dozens of drawings, diagrams, and schematics, including Kiesler's 1942 design for Peggy Guggenheim's Art of This Century gallery, on West 57th Street in New York. These documents reflect the extension of Kiesler's design approach to and activation of objects and spaces – in this case, reanimating art and the ways

Some of the documents, which show Kiesler's ideas for activating objects and spaces, were "liberated" from the walls. Photo: Kris Graves.

humans perceive it. These drawings were the most delightfully strange, fantastical, and future casting in the exhibition, showing ways artworks can be liberated from static viewing. Other documents presented his design for the Vision Machine, a sort of mad scientist's apparatus, conceived to visualize human sight and the electrical transmissions in the brain that make it all possible.

In each room, Wasiuta's curatorial presence was a gentle but consistent force. The Mobile Home Library possessed a particular gravitas, a hypnotic machine that was active even when the viewer/user was not. The cyclical vitrines that held the Laboratory's work activated the contents under the glass, making new associations visible as the four rotating panels slowly moved. The overwhelming number of drawings for the Art of This Century gallery, which Wasiuta called Exhibition Machines, were arranged in more white powder-coated steel and glass vitrines, six of which were anchored to poles that stretched vertically from the ceiling to the floor and pierced the central space of the room. This arrangement activated the room and invited the viewer to wander *through* it rather than parade listlessly *around* its perimeter.

Frederick Kiesler, Study for Vision Machine (The Shortcoming of Human Sight), Part 1 of 2, 1938. Ink on paper, 21 by 28 centimeters. © Austrian Frederick and Lillian Kiesler Private Foundation, Vienna.

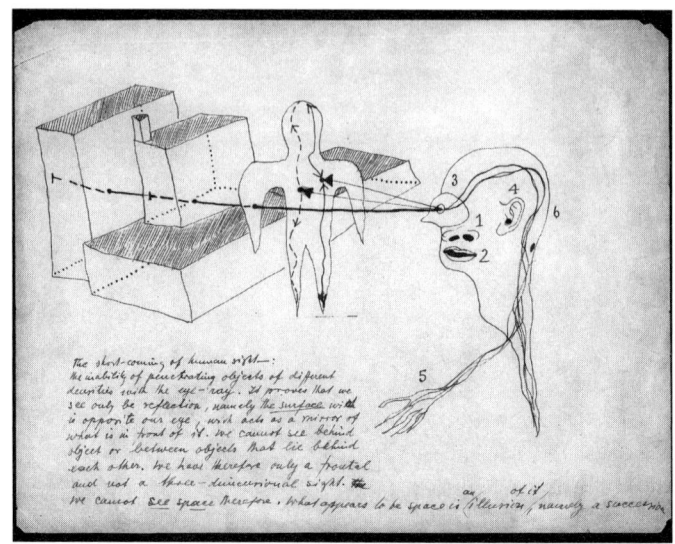

The sort of multivalent practice of a figure like Kiesler is more common among academic-practitioner architects today, but in his time, he was anomalous, peerless, even "prescient." His Laboratory of Design Correlation reminds me of Muriel Cooper's Visible Language Workshop of the 1980s, in which she and students at MIT pioneered interface design and information systems. This experimental approach to design also relates to the blending of architectural structure and mediated screen space in Elizabeth Diller's early work. In this sense, the exhibition's gambit (and indeed Kiesler's) is instructive for practitioners today. *Design* is a verb – a practice, thought process, an investigation. What is engineered, built, or constructed is merely a tangible result of those interrelated activities. In this light, the exhibition spoke to two meanings of *vision* as it relates to Kiesler: seeing and idea. Despite the technical accomplishment of the Mobile Home Library and the beauty of the armatures that displayed all of this material, it was the primacy of the drawing that ultimately activated this show. Drawing embodies Kiesler's total vision. Here, a drawing is as significant as the formal outcome, if not more so, because it is a raw and unfettered rendering of an idea.

Ben Fehrman-Lee is a graphic designer, typographer, and art director who develops projects with individuals and institutions for culture and commerce. He is an associate design director at 2×4 in New York and also maintains an independent practice focused on editorial and typographic projects across media.

Lina Malfona

All the Colors Between Black And White

The Venice Biennale is a real and virtual place where micronarratives and nanostories, often purpose-built, are mounted and exhibited for a few months in the Giardini and the Arsenale. But beyond these gates, the Biennale's exhibitions also serve as an amplifier for a series of collateral shows. On the occasion of the 60th Art Biennale, which runs through November 24, 2024, the Los Angeles County Museum of Art (LACMA) has mounted "Zeng Fanzhi: Near and Far/Now and Then" in the Scuola Grande di Santa Maria della Misericordia, in the Cannaregio district. Cocurated by Michael Govan, the director of LACMA, and Stephen Little, the museum's curator of Chinese art, the show is not only a dialogue between art and architecture but also between two masters of form: Zeng Fanzhi, a Beijing-based painter known for making monumental canvases that traverse abstraction and figuration, and Tadao Ando, an Osaka-based self-taught architect of dramatic interiors often defined by light. Reading Andrew Maerkle's April article in the *New York Times*, which includes excerpts from a conversation between Ando and Zeng before the making of the exhibition,[1] it is clear that the two authors are both interested in the fusion of classical and modern, Eastern and Western sensibilities, which guided the show's design.

    The physical dialogue between the two authors' works takes place in a highly characterized and layered architectural space far from the large crowds at the Biennale, which certainly conditioned Ando's intervention. Home to one of Venice's most venerable confraternities, the Scuola Grande is a Roman classicism building, essentially like a Roman basilica, and thus quite out of scale with the Venetian fabric. Built in the 14th century, the hall was renovated by Jacopo Sansovino, beginning in 1532, and its new interior inaugurated in 1583, after his death. To overcome decades of misuse, the building was, again, given a new life by Venice-based TA Architettura, in 2015, after an unrealized restoration project by Gianni Fabbri. The historic hall, which now has black steel

1. See Andrew Maerkle, "Match Made in Venice: Tadao Ando and Zeng Fanzhi," *New York Times*, April 15, 2024, https://www.nytimes.com/2024/04/15/arts/design/ando-fangzhi-art-architecture-venice-biennale.html.

flooring with a reflective calamine finish, gained the flexibility to host exhibitions and events.

The reflective quality of the floor enhances the aura of Zeng's new oil paintings, the result of the artist's decades-long research on color theory. In our age of renderings and photorealism, Zeng induces us to recognize the superiority of painting, which he understands as an active practice of research that collides with the materiality of the world: colors, smells, and textures, the tactility and grain of materials, and our relationship to perspective, from near and far, thus breaking out of the flatness of the screen. Drawing from impressionist and pointillist practices, Zeng creates images that emerge through strategic dabs of color, but these have nothing to do with pixels. Like Claire Falkenstein's iron and colored-glass entrance gate at the Peggy Guggenheim Collection in Venice, Zeng's canvases are characterized by a tangle of lines that compose figures that are easily recognizable from a distance, but when viewed up close, they dissolve into pure color, or rather a weave of colors generated by his layers of brushstrokes.[2]

On the ground floor of the Scuola Grande – a large hall divided into a nave and two aisles by Corinthian columns – a conversation between two 4.8-by-4.8-meter paintings, *Non-Self* and *Ephemerality* (both dated 2019–23), occurs in the kind of spiritual space that Ando handles so well. By mounting the two paintings so that they face each other from the nave's two ends, Ando creates a space dense with connections rather than empty. Similar to his other projects, where a dialogue takes place between distant objects, the two paintings generate force fields, so the viewer does not stand in the center but rather is drawn to one end or the other. On the second floor, the architect guides the visitor through the space perhaps even more decisively. Here, he designed a series of freestanding parallel walls almost the width of the room, cutting progressively larger apertures in each plane to create a perspectival composition. The openings visually link the different sections of the show, acting as windows that allow the visitor to enjoy a broad view of the exhibition. There is a moment when the openings themselves read as paintings, perfectly framing Zeng's work. However, the viewer must zigzag through the partitions, walking the entire length of each wall before reaching the largest painting in the show. Throughout the exhibition, Ando seems to be asserting that his installation – the architecture – cannot be a neutral field. The overall effect of the installation is the result of an equal confrontation

2. See Gladys Chung, ed., *Zeng Fanzhi: Catalogue Raisonné*, vol. 1 (Milan: Skira, 2020); cf. Zeng Fanzhi, Stephen Little, Barbara Pollack, Carter Ratcliff, eds., *Zeng Fanzhi* (Zurich: Hauser & Wirth Publishers, 2023).
3. See Lina Malfona, "Museo di Punta della Dogana, Venezia | Punta della Dogana Contemporary Art Centre, Venice," *L'Industria delle Costruzioni* 411 (January–February 2010): 88–97.
4. See Anne Stenne, ed., *Pierre Huyghe: Liminal* (Venice: Marsilio Arte, 2024).
5. Jun'ichirō Tanizaki, *In Praise of Shadows* (New Haven: Leete's Island Books, 1977), 20–22. Quoted in Kenneth Frampton, ed., *Tadao Ando* (New York: The Museum of Modern Art, 1991), 13.

The first floor of "Zeng Fanzhi: Near and Far/Now and Then," April 17 – September 30, 2024, Scuola Grande Della Misericordia, Venice. Organized by the Los Angeles County Museum of Art. All photos: Stefan Altenburger Photography Zurich. © Zeng Fanzhi.

between the artist and the architect. Ando's imposing white walls contrast with and thus enhance Zeng's vibrant color palette without obscuring the Misericordia's frescoed walls.

In comparison, at the mouth of the Grand Canal, at the Museum at Punta della Dogana, which Ando restored for the Pinault Foundation, in 2009, the walls disappear into the darkness.[3] Punta della Dogana is currently showing "Liminal," an exhibition of recent work by Pierre Huyghe.[4] In those gloomy, dark rooms, Huyghe's works appear phantasmagoric, as the architecture is eclipsed by the portentous installations. One wonders if softening the light and choosing a darker color for the walls of the Misericordia installation would have enhanced Zeng's vibrant canvases even more. However, if Ando had tempered his design, he wouldn't have established a dialogue between the art and architecture, and he would have failed to establish a relationship between the artist and the viewer. And he probably would have also betrayed himself. The coherence of Ando's thought is indeed out of step with the present sentiment, with its tendency toward self-flattery and moralism. Ando decided to enhance the artist's work while guiding the visitor along his path and providing vantage points that allow the viewer to engage with the work.

Above and opposite page: The second floor of "Zeng Fanzhi: Near and Far/Now and Then." The diagonal wall marks the entrance. © Zeng Fanzhi.

Lina Malfona is associate professor of architectural theory and design at the University of Pisa, the founder of the office Malfona Petrini Architecture (MPA), and the director of polit(t)ico research lab.

Toward the back of the exhibition, there is a sacellum, a small room that houses precious works. On display are drawings Zeng made with graphite, chalk, colored pigments, and gold dust on handmade paper and signed in pencil. Made from 2015 to 2021, these works recall the tradition of Chinese landscape drawings. Subjects range from the iconography of Adam and Eve to the Crucifixion, from cloudy mountains to rocks and old trees. While some recall symbols in traditional Chinese culture, others speak a universal language and are composed of multiple drawings, often vertical, like a polyptych. This *Wunderkammer*, also designed by Ando, contains Zeng's most intimate works. It is a precious space analogous to the small library of precious volumes Michelangelo designed as the third and last room of his Laurentian Library, in Florence. As is often the case, the treasure lies in the secret room and not in the grand hall.

If on the ground floor and in the sacellum Ando shares the stage and lets the artworks speak, on the upper floor he does not relinquish his authorship. The intent is to illustrate Zeng's work, guide the viewer, and create a contemplative environment sheltered from external disturbances. In this sense, Ando's introduction of a singular diagonal wall, which denotes the entrance area while protecting the exhibition space from the noise of visitors climbing the stairs, is meaningful. The diagonal wall creates a threshold and a space of decompression that precedes one's immersion in the visual experience of the exhibition. This is a frequent motif in Ando's work, starting with the Church of the Light, one of his earliest and best-known buildings. This wall has a dual role, like all of Ando's walls, separating as much as it captures, directing light as much as it creates darkness. It is a ritual wall that can be likened to a ceremonial act.

In the end, all of Ando's actions are defined by the interaction of light and shadow. As he has repeatedly said, we need to rediscover the depth and richness of darkness, because it is precisely on the border between brightness and darkness that objects take shape. Ando's installation begins in the darkness of the ground floor and then continues in the artificial light of the upper floor. But unlike Huyghe's show, the darkness handled by Ando is not performative; it is not a scenic artifice. For Ando, darkness is an existential, cognitive, and human condition before it is a formal one. As Japanese novelist Jun'ichirō Tanizaki writes, "Here in the darkness immutable tranquility holds sway."[5] Clearly, for Ando, architecture is an act of intellectual integrity.

Observations on a View

The relationship between spatial access and class positioning has been a subject visited by countless architects, artists, and theorists throughout history. Artist Nikita Gale adds to this discussion with a recent show at Petzel Gallery titled "NOSEBLEED." The installation used motifs of stadium seating to question the notion that the highest seats in the house are also somehow the most disadvantaged despite their far-reaching view of both the sporting action and other attendees. The floor of the room was covered with a large-scale print of an AI-generated stadium view that was then reflected in giant mirrored panels that stretched from floor to ceiling on an oblique angle. As a result, those who entered the installation were immediately situated in a simulated nosebleed seat, looking down at framed photographs on the floor in much the same manner that a spectator looks down at a sporting event. The frames contain images of stadiums from a bird's-eye view and close-up images of Gale's ear, eye, and mouth, emphasizing the importance of sight and sound in a stadium environment. The most notable pieces were the scale models that dotted the floor, made up of Frankensteined elements from Madison Square Garden and

Nikita Gale, "NOSEBLEED," Petzel Gallery, New York, May 2 – June 8, 2024. © Petzel.

Manchester Arena, as well as two unbuilt fascist projects: Albert Speer's Deutsches Stadion and Gaetano Ciocca's Theatre of the Masses. Through these models, Gale exhibits a clear understanding of the power of architecture to create and curate views, a subject that architects are undoubtedly familiar with in the context of discussions surrounding high-rise towers and view corridors. This aspect of Gale's work makes it important as an adjacent contribution to architectural discourse.

– D. Joseph Dignan

Jimenez Lai

Swings, Stacks, and Spools at Coachella

How useful is a folly? Today, the folly is a rare site for full-scale architectural experimentation. While architects are forming larger questions, a typical building commission may not always be the best platform to explore new ideas. Such investigations may need to take place at smaller scales: models, furniture, drawings, diagrams, and details, or, on a lucky day, a 1:1 folly that can test an idea that the world is not yet ready for.

Goldenvoice, the company that operates the annual Coachella Valley Music and Arts Festival, hired bright-eyed curators, Paul Clemente and Raffi Lehrer, who, since 2015, have used this platform to seek out people working on architectural experiments. The Coachella installations function as landmarks for photo opportunities, as meeting points for friends to find one another, as well as shading devices. In 2015, Ball-Nogues Studio transformed paper pulp into a structurally stable material; in 2017, Chiaozza precisely scaled up the effects of imprecision by gathering lumpy handcrafted models into a forest of colorful creatures at the size of small buildings; in 2022, the vegetal furs of Oana Stănescu's dog statues provoked questions about greenness as well as the Venturi, Scott Brown duck by covering flat, animal-shaped billboards with plants; and in my own case, in 2016, I worked on how posture may be studied as a structural problem through an oversized contrapposto figure.

In 2024, the curators commissioned three full-scale follies for Coachella: Morag Myerscough designed a kinetic architecture that swings; Nebbia created a sensorial experience that stacks; and HANNAH produced a 3D-printed breakthrough that spools. Each project posed contemporary questions about the field: Can buildings move? How immersive can projections be? What are the current limits of digital fabrication technology? In each case, an architectural idea was able to be pushed forward.

Swings
Myerscough, a London-based artist, helped examine the status of kinetic architecture with her entry Dancing in the Sky.

Morag Myerscough, Dancing in the Sky, April 12 – April 21, 2024, Coachella Valley Music and Arts Festival, Coachella Valley, California. Photos: Lance Gerber.

Morag Myerscough, sketch of Dancing in the Sky, 2024. Drawing courtesy the artist.

Can architecture move, or rather, can a static building have enough moving components to suggest an architecture in motion? The desire to move entire buildings can be seen in the walking steampunk castle in Hayao Miyazaki's *Howl's Moving Castle* and in A Walking City by Archigram, both of which suggest that kinetic architecture requires entire buildings to walk. Rather than suggest a fully mobile architecture, Myerscough isolates only key fragments of a stationary elevation to be in constant and fluttering motion. Whereas Theo Jansen's *strandbeests* are entire sculptures that walk using passive wind power, the idea of a building with many kinetic parts has always been subtly expressed within the conventions of architecture. Case in point, the quarter circles that architects draw in plans to indicate door swings are evidence that almost every building has an abundance of moveable parts. Vito Acconci and Steven Holl's 1993 Storefront for Art and Architecture in New York, for example, is an architecture whose primary feature is its rotating facade. In Myerscough's folly, the swinging shapes flap back and forth like banners designed to silently signal a gathering point over a long distance. Furthermore, the elevation of Dancing in the Sky suggests a solid-void reversal, where only the windows are solids. An oblique projection of the swinging panels in midmotion is echoed in the isometric graphic patterns on the stationary surfaces.

Stacks

In architecture, a brick problem is a thought exercise in stacking, especially if the additive components are self-similar. A brick problem may not necessarily be about actual bricks – it could be about a stack of modular parts in a range of shapes, sizes, inhabitability, or function. From Moshe Safdie's Habitat 67 to Greg Lynn's BlobWall, a brick problem expands the concept of stackable units as well as the relationship between them. The London architecture firm Nebbia, founded by Brando Posocco and Madhav Kidao, advanced the idea of stacking through an aggregation of large U-shaped "bricks" made of steel frames clad in plywood. Can a stack be an experience from both up close and afar? Can the cavity under a pile of bricks be both occupiable and stage a space of sensations? Nebbia helped answer both questions through their installation, called Babylon. Coachella, a sweltering environment during the day, is unlike most other outdoor festivals as the harsh desert sun has a bleaching effect on the outdoor experience. Nebbia's pyramidal stack produced two contrasting atmospheres: a muted exterior and a kaleidoscopic

Nebbia, isonometric diagram of Babylon, Coachella, 2024. Drawing courtesy the architects.

interior. The gray cellulose pulp on the exterior is a consistent and uniform finish that renders the stack as a low-resolution mass when seen from a distance. Inside, however, the pyramid becomes a shaded cave with tiny tunnel views of the sky. As a slightly cooler and darker space, this interior serves as a multimedia environment for light shows and other videos that are projected on the walls. Slivers of sunlight stream in through the cracks between the U-shaped bricks, interacting with the artificial lighting from the projections.

Spools
A spool is a device onto which a continuous coiling of an uninterrupted line can be reeled. Although typically cylindrical, any shape can be considered a spool if an unbroken thread is coiled around it. In 3D printing, the void around which the solids are printed can be considered a conceptual spool. The Ithaca, New York–based design duo HANNAH, Leslie Lok and Sasa Zivkovic, produced Monarchs: A House in Six Parts, a group of digitally fabricated concrete spools the size of buildings. In 2019, prior to this project, HANNAH built the 3D-printed, single-room Ashen Cabin. What sets Monarchs apart from Ashen Cabin is the breakthrough in the size and the scale of fabrication. Although Ashen Cabin is a small building, each 3D-printed component of the cabin is at the furniture scale. The foundation of the cabin is a bundle of nine 3D-printed parts, each no larger than 36 inches in any direction. In other words, the foundation is a collection of nine small spools. The size of a print is constrained by several factors: the size of the print bed, the length of the crane arm, the carrying capacity of the available vehicles, the weight of the components, and the cure time of the concrete. However, in the five years since Ashen Cabin, HANNAH has managed to enlarge the print size of a spool exponentially.

Digital fabrications, since the 1990s, have often been experiments in exporting vector lines from a computer to the built environment. How the vector line subtracts or adds material has been the key issue in every serious conversation within the field. Unlike the subtractive logic of the laser cutter or CNC milling, 3D printing is an additive logic. It is far more difficult to control the material texture, line thickness, sharpness of corners, and most important, printable area with an additive logic. While 3D printers have been widely available since the late 2000s, the printable volume has basically remained at the size of a small model. For Coachella, HANNAH accomplished a massive upgrade in the size of a single spool. Whereas the

Nebbia, Babylon, Coachella, 2024. Interior photo: Lance Gerber.
Exterior photo: Alberto Sinigaglia.

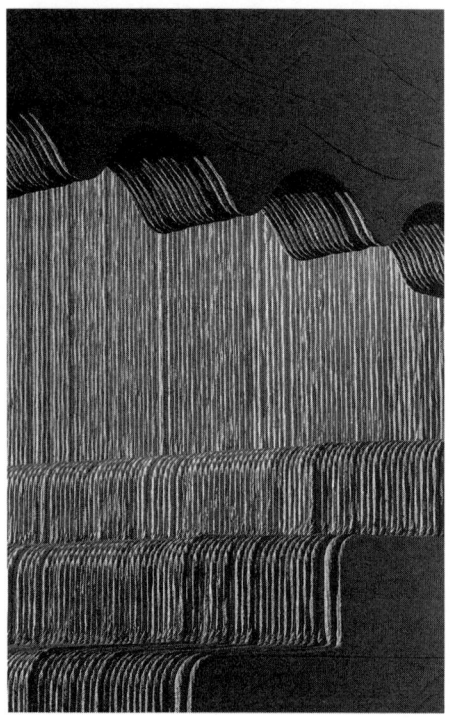

HANNAH, Monarchs: A House in Six Parts, Coachella, 2024. Photos: James Florio. Top photo: Lance Gerber.

HANNAH, Ashen Cabin, Ithaca, New York, 2019. Photo: Andy Chen.

Ashen Cabin spools were useable as chairs, Monarchs' chunks were more like rooms. The printed concrete was a comfortable thermal mass come nightfall, and during the day, the 70-foot-tall wood structures above the 3D-printed bases provided additional shade from the intense desert sun.

As this year's "follies" demonstrated, Coachella has emerged as a rare platform for full-scale architectural experimentation. The Young Architects Program at MoMA PS1 in New York ended in 2019, and the Serpentine Pavilion in London is typically reserved for architects further along in their careers. Organizations such as Art Omi in Ghent, New York; Materials & Applications in Los Angeles; MMCA in Seoul; X-Site in Taipei; and the Ragdale Ring in Lake Forest, Illinois, still offer opportunities to realize full-scale follies. What sets Coachella apart from these institutions is the size of its audience and the experimentation the curators allow. Given its popularity, Coachella is uniquely positioned to support ambitious projects by allowing open-ended inquiries to take form. In 2024, there were new lessons in how to swing, stack, and spool, but each year, we can collectively ask new questions to be tested in the desert. Such projects transform ideas into precedents, furthering subsequent works on the same problems. And that may be the ultimate usefulness – and value – of a folly.

Jimenez Lai works at Bureau Spectacular and teaches at USC. He was the 2024 Gwathmey Chair at The Cooper Union.

Observations on Quick Books

"Architectural writing is not like the writing of history or of poetry," Vitruvius claims in Book 5 of his Ten Books on Architecture. *"Histories by their very nature maintain the interest of their readers, they present the ever-changing anticipation of learning something new. With poems, on the other hand, it is the meters, the feet, and the elegant placement of words . . . that carry our interest."* Warning that the generally unfamiliar language of architecture is obfuscating, he continues, *"Unless the wide-ranging writings of authorities on [architecture] have been condensed and expressed in a few, crystal-clear sentences, the density of the prose, not to mention the sheer length of it, confuses readers' minds."*

There is no confusion in Lydia Kallipoliti's Histories of Ecological Design: An Unfinished Cyclopedia or in Jeanne Gang's The Art of Architectural Grafting. Kallipoliti's fast-paced histories are indeed charged with the possibilities of learning something new, and Gang introduces architectural concepts through terms any gardener would understand. And both books are easy reads, even quick books. In fact, at her book launch at the Cooper Union in April, Kallipoliti said she wrote for the short attention span of today's readers, which might be why I sometimes wanted a deeper

Recommended reading: Lydia Kallipoliti, *Histories of Ecological Design: An Unfinished Cyclopedia*. Actar, 2024. 279 pages. Jeanne Gang, *The Art of Architectural Grafting*. Park Books, 2024. 180 pages.

history. But the book is, after all, a "cyclopedia," a heady inventory of ecological thinking over the past 150 years, with a bibliography certain to ignite readers' curiosity and propel future research.

Gang's brief autobiographical interludes, tucked between longer chapters on grafting techniques, aren't quite poetry, but they do give breathing room to a book dense with text and images, the latter illustrating methods of grafting in both horticulture and Studio Gang's projects. The result is surprisingly refreshing, a subtle yet highly effective approach to rethinking how to make architecture in the face of climate change. While Kallipoliti represents the scholarly research arm of architecture today, Gang represents ecologically minded practice. Should Kallipoliti's "unfinished" cyclopedia be updated someday, one can imagine Gang's concept of grafting will be a succinct new entry.

– Cynthia Davidson

Todd Gannon

Remembering José Oubrerie

José Oubrerie (1932–2024). Image courtesy the Knowlton School, The Ohio State University.

José Oubrerie, one of the most talented architects and impactful educators of his generation, died on March 9, 2024, at the age of 91.

In a career that spanned seven decades, Oubrerie moved from the École nationale supérieure des Beaux-Arts, in Paris, to an apprenticeship in Le Corbusier's famous atelier at 35 rue de Sèvres to private practice in Europe and then in the United States, producing a small but impressive portfolio comprised almost exclusively of masterpieces. His signal achievements – the French Cultural Center in Damascus; the Miller House in Lexington, Kentucky; and the completion of Le Corbusier's church of Saint-Pierre, in Firminy – each bear the mark of his mentor's influence, but, more important, they demonstrate Oubrerie's own inventiveness, his irrepressible mischievousness, and his refusal to play the part of dutiful protégé. A legendary teacher at schools in Paris, Milan, New York, Chicago, and at the University of Kentucky, where he was dean of the college of architecture from 1987 to 1991, and Ohio State, where he chaired the architecture program from 1991 to 1997, Oubrerie instilled in several generations of students his infectious enthusiasm for great design and a disdain for gutless conventionality perhaps best captured in his distinctive pronunciation of the word *sheetrock*.

When I met José, in the summer of 1993, I knew nothing of his storied past and legendary pedigree. All I knew was that this elegantly rumpled man with a thick French accent was willing to look past my inauspicious transcript (which had caused an admissions officer understandable concern) and admit me to Ohio State's undergraduate architecture program based on my portfolio, which he flipped through and deemed, with a characteristic shrug, "pretty good."

A year later, I took an eye-opening studio with him. This was a heady time to be at Ohio State, where instructors like Doug Graf and Jeff Kipnis – whose brilliance did not derive from verbal brevity – loomed large. José's teaching, by contrast, was devoid of complex jargon and elaborate theoretical justification. Instead, he delivered criticism on a sliding scale of mostly one-word assessments. The best projects were simply "Great!" and

Oubrerie adds ideograms to the exhibition, "The Chapel of the Mosquitoes," SCI-Arc, Los Angeles, 2017. Photo: Todd Gannon.

the worst ones "Terrible." And though he required all students to have an idea (pronounced *eye-DEE*), these only mattered as instantiated in working models, which were to be elaborated throughout the semester with whatever materials were at hand.

In his studio, two classmates and I built a large plywood site model, roughly four by eight feet, and then set to work populating its surfaces with roughly assembled chipboard constructions. As models proliferated, we produced piles of scraps and rejected components that we kept in a cardboard box beneath the model. When José came in, he'd perch himself on a stool, look carefully at our progress, and then bellow, "Bring me the box," which he'd root through for bits and pieces he could use to make improvements. Sometimes, he'd even tear a section from one student's model and attach it, inevitably in a different orientation, to someone else's project. In just a few minutes of rough revision, he'd seize and exploit latent possibilities, clean up and intensify formal complexities, and our clumsy piles of chipboard would begin to come to life. Then, just as things were beginning to click, he'd put down his scissors, turn to us, and intone, "You see, it could be good, but you must work!"

It took me a while to realize that José's teaching, which sometimes seemed maddeningly open-ended, involved cunning acts of intellectual generosity. He'd lay down just enough hints to keep you going, but he'd never just hand you an answer. A crit with José was always a provocation. He'd demonstrate that what you were doing could be done, but he'd leave it to you to discover and deliver the coup de grâce.

Oubrerie's teaching mirrored his own design method and drew on his early training and apprenticeship with Le Corbusier. As a young man, he studied painting in his hometown of Nantes, then relocated to Paris to make his way as a painter in the mid-1950s. Life as a struggling artist moved him to enroll in architecture school, but he quickly became disillusioned with the program at the École. On the recommendation of a family friend, he found work on the construction site of Le Corbusier's Maison du Brésil, and soon suspended his studies to dedicate himself to an apprenticeship with the architect. Over the next several years, Oubrerie immersed himself in Le Corbusier's theories and method, internalizing the proportional logic of the Modulor and adopting his mentor's habit of capturing design concepts in broad-stroked ideograms and quickly assembled sketch models, such as those Oubrerie completed while developing the Firminy church in the early 1960s.

Le Corbusier and Oubrerie, Church of Saint-Pierre de Firminy-Vert, Firminy, France, 2006. Photo: Olivier Martin-Gambier. Courtesy Fondation Le Corbusier.

Soon after Corbusier's death, in 1965, Oubrerie and another apprentice, Guillermo Jullian de la Fuente, formed a partnership in hopes – soon dashed – of seeing Le Corbusier's Venice Hospital and other projects through to completion. In 1967, he established his own Paris-based atelier, and within a few years he managed to get the Firminy church moving again. Construction finally commenced, in 1973, and proceeded sporadically before stalling, with little more than the building's square base completed, in 1979.

By then, Oubrerie had begun developing the French Cultural Center in a series of rough paper models and loose sketches that slowly tightened into the scheme's spiraling interior and a complex facade with which he paid homage to Le Corbusier's late-career achievements in béton brut (such as in Chandigarh, on which Oubrerie worked), trading the master's deeply shadowed grillwork for crisply patterned

José Oubrerie, chocolate bar study model of the Miller House, 1991. Opposite page: Miller House, Lexington, Kentucky, 1991. South facade. Photo by Samuel Ludwig. Photos courtesy the author.

planarity. At the Miller House, commissioned after he relocated permanently to the United States in the mid-1980s, Oubrerie again unsettled his Corbusian training, assembling a masterful ménage out of Le Corbusier's five points, American stick framing, and historical and contemporary references he sampled with the erudition of Nikolaus Pevsner and the wry insouciance of the Beastie Boys. Conceiving the house as a three-dimensional village for the Millers and their two grown children, Oubrerie arranged three wood cabins, connected by steel catwalks, that hover over a communal ground floor. At the perimeter, massive concrete facades stand guard against the encroaching suburban development he derided as "l'ennemi." Improvising much of the house's intricate detailing well after construction had commenced, Oubrerie never produced a complete set of working drawings. Instead, he developed the scheme in a torrent of sketches and study models, including a now legendary one crafted from bars of chocolate!

Throughout these years, the Firminy church languished as a modern ruin. When funding from the French government finally came, in 2001, Oubrerie enlisted a small team of French architects, including Romain Chazalon, who relocated to Columbus, Ohio, to work directly with him to develop digital documents. Construction began again, in 2003, and was completed to great acclaim in 2006.

In contrast to the planar complexity in Damascus and the elemental intensity in Lexington, the Firminy church offers a spare interior volume that is nothing short of sublime. Though Oubrerie stayed true to Corbusier's initial intentions, technical and programmatic demands necessitated small but impactful changes. Most significant, the sacristy and priests' quarters at the base of the building were reconceived as a small

museum, in keeping with funding requirements. As realized, the building weaves together secular and sacred spaces that rise from a complex composition of concrete, glass, and steel at the ground level to a transcendent volume above defined by the play of light across otherwise unadorned concrete surfaces.

The opening of the church brought Oubrerie waves of attention in the form of awards, exhibitions, lecture invitations, and publications, but new commissions mostly eluded him. In his later years, he turned his attention back to painting, and, in 2015, he exhibited a suite of canvases alongside an as-yet-unrealized proposal for a small chapel on the grounds of Steven Holl's 'T' Space gallery, in Rhinebeck, New York. A few years later, he and his wife, Cicely, relocated to a beautifully appointed loft in Lexington, where they maintained their habit of hosting exquisite dinner parties for lucky guests until the end.

I last saw José a few months before he died. The lunch we planned extended into afternoon coffee, then a bottle of rosé, and eventually dinner, with wine and gossip flowing well into the evening. Though his movement had slowed and his burly frame had shrunk considerably, José otherwise remained as I'd always known him – gregarious and hilarious, fearlessly opinionated, and smart as a whip. With his passing, our field has lost a gifted architect, a beloved mentor, and a dear friend, whose brilliant work lives on as a testament to his uncompromising commitment to the art of architecture and, as important, to a life well-lived.

Todd Gannon is a professor of architecture at The Ohio State University. His most recent books are *Figments of the Architectural Imagination* (2022) and *Franklin D. Israel: A Life in Architecture* (forthcoming in 2025).

Observations on Capsules

The Nakagin Capsule Tower, designed by Kisho Kurokawa and constructed in 1972, was torn down in 2022. Following more than a decade of deliberation, the demolition put an end to worsening living conditions, ongoing structural decay, and the old dreams of the building's semi-obsessive fanbase, comprised mostly of its final residents. Tatsuyuki Maeda was one such resident, a man who, by the time of the tower's demolition, owned 12 capsules. He even rented two neighboring apartments just to watch and film the razing.

Maeda is a man driven by love. Last year, I accompanied a group of students and professors to a warehouse on the outskirts of Tokyo, where I learned that Maeda had managed to buy 11 more capsules, bringing his total to 23. At the warehouse, we witnessed Maeda's passion project in full effect. One capsule was entirely refinished, its every detail restored, down to the original stereo system, television, and telephone. Although the technology is long outdated, it was hard not to see it as a futuristic image. Today, 16 of Maeda's capsules have been refinished and shipped off for exhibition in venues ranging from the San Francisco Museum of Modern Art to SHUTL gallery

The Nakagin Capsule Preservation and Restoration Project warehouse, Tokyo, Japan. Photo: Stanley Spence.

in Tokyo, just a 10-minute walk from the tower's original location. The seven remaining capsules, in various states of (dis)repair, are patiently waiting to become objects of affection like their already-restored siblings. According to Maeda, the plan is to create a seaside "capsule village" in Japan's Kanagawa prefecture, in which these capsules will be available for rent through Airbnb. Whatever the result, Maeda is determined to bring the capsules back into use. He is, after all, a man driven by love.

– Stanley Spence

André Patrão

The Language Of the End Of Architecture

1. A Kaleidoscope of Endless Wordplay

"The end of architecture" is a menacing pronouncement with a long history. It recurs in different guises and preserves an ominous attractive force in every instance. Even before we make sense of what the expression means, what it entails, what it critiques, or what it shows, we're first enthralled by its ambiguity and its potential for wordplay. *End* has many meanings. The equivocacies and the slippages from one sense to another conjure a never-ending stream of connections, tensions, and contradictions that tempt us to look closer.

As a verb, *end* refers to an act, "to end"; as a noun, *end* stands for either "an end" among many or a singular, final "the end." It conveys the cessation of something's existence or of an aspect of something's existence, as in "demise," "destruction," or "extinction." It can be violently executed, as in "abolishing" or "killing," or can take place naturally and predictably, as in "expiration" or "terminus," or bring a process to a fulfilling totality in its "culmination" or "completion." It sets an aspiration to be achieved, as in a "goal" or "objective." It suggests a boundary to which something is circumscribed, as in a "limit" of its extent. It may even point to an extremity, like a "tip" or "tail." The phrase "means to an end" forges an interdependency between an objective and the manner in which to attain it. We yearn for something to be over and something else to come, "the light at the end of the tunnel." We clamor for something to cease, "Will this never end?" We fear destruction when we hear "the end is near!" Not all extremities hold the same moral value in "the wrong end of the stick," which returns us to the word's original etymological meaning as something "in front of." Yet, today, we can just as well find it on a "backend"! We don't give it much importance, though, when it's lost among "odds and ends." Things are said to have "a beginning and an end," and the latter is often found at "the end of the line," but these rules of geometry don't apply when we describe the hardship of "making ends meet."

The latter idiom's contested origin could lie in the French *joindre les deux bouts*, in which *bouts* (tips) is homonymous with *buts* (goals). In fact, the French language reveals a whole new set of connections in the etymological roots of English words, since *end* translates as *fin*. *Finally* promises a conclusion, or celebrates its arrival. *Finitude*, an inevitable expiration, is bestowed on things with the adjective *finite*. The expression *à la fin* (in the end) reduces things to what they ultimately boil down to. But there is no direct translation for *enfin*, a standalone expression uttered almost onomatopoeically to signal the exhaustion of a topic, or our exhaustion in talking about it, the latter concluding but not necessarily completing our discourse about it.

Should we, with an *enfin*, end this endless line of ends with an endpoint? For there seems to be no end in sight to the ends of the word *end*… other than being at our wit's end! Plunged into wordplay, we unfold and refold the same word into copies of itself, splintering its meanings and reconnecting them in intricate patterns. The result is a kaleidoscope of significations that is semantically revealing but also potentially deceiving. Baffled by what we see, we may believe we are struggling with the complexities of thinking about the "end" of things. In fact, we are merely caught up in linguistic confusion. Wordplay traps our thoughts in what comes down to a matter of language: simply put, *end* has many meanings.

"Philosophy is a battle against the bewitchment of our intelligence by means of language."[1] So says Ludwig Wittgenstein, the philosopher known among architects for taking part in the design of a house for his sister, but whose major philosophical contributions remain largely undiscussed in architecture. In his early writing, he claims there is a direct correspondence between the world as we understand it and a logically structured language with which we refer to it. This view does not reduce everything to a logical fact but limits the reach of language, as he conceived it, to logical facts. Wittgenstein scolds philosophers for the misuse of language in this regard, and accuses them of embarking on nonsensical pursuits when trying to use language to pin down ideas that are beyond it. Ethics, aesthetics, metaphysics, and religion, for example, cannot be explained by language as if they were logical facts. He thus deems philosophical problems in these subjects as expressions of the misuse of language. In Wittgenstein's ascetic view, philosophy should simply clarify what can be spoken of, and distinguish it from what cannot. "The right method of philosophy," he writes in *Tractatus*

---

1. Ludwig Wittgenstein, *Philosophical Investigations*, trans. G. E. M. Anscombe (1934; repr., Oxford: Blackwell, 2001), para. 109.

Logico-Philosophicus, "would be this: to say nothing except what can be said . . . and then always, when someone else wished to say something metaphysical, to demonstrate to him that he had given no meaning to certain signs in his propositions. This method would be unsatisfying to the other . . . but it would be the only strictly correct method."[2]

Wittgenstein's later writings correct and reject many of the premises and conclusions of the *Tractatus*. His conception of language shifts toward the way we *use* it. Meaning, he argues, lies first and foremost in the way we employ language. Words or sequences of words are meaningful insofar as they elicit certain reaction from us, which depend on the socially accepted linguistic rules of the contexts in which they're used. As for Wittgenstein's earlier prescriptions for philosophy, he not only stands by them but enforces them. Whichever topic he turns his attention to, he seeks to release his audience from the traps of misusing or misinterpreting language. As he famously put it: "What is your aim in philosophy? – To show the fly the way out of the fly-bottle."[3]

In *Philosophical Investigations*, Wittgenstein develops a painstaking case-by-case analysis of our use of language and our assumptions about it. This clarifying activity often begins with the same fundamental question: "What does it mean to say that the 'is' in 'The rose is red' has a different meaning from the 'is' in 'twice two is four?'";[4] "What does it mean to say 'What is happening now has significance' or 'has deep significance'?";[5] "What does it mean to say: 'If I mean something by it, surely it must make sense?'"[6] His questions do not seek an essentialist determination of what each word or expression signifies. Instead, they call for nothing more than a *description* of the way we use them. And the answers to these questions do not lie beyond language. For Wittgenstein, we think in language, and understand our thinking by looking at our use of language.

So, what does it mean to say "the end of architecture?"

2. An Interplay of Telos and Death

In 1992, in Wittgenstein's hometown, the Vienna Architecture Conference convened for a discussion provocatively titled *The End of Architecture?* In the book that came out of the event, the organizer Peter Noever paints a grim picture of a situation in which "architects who attempt to practice real architecture" are threatened by "reactionary trends . . . springing up everywhere; there has been a tacit declaration of war against architecture."[7] Coop Himmelblau attacks a form

2. Ludwig Wittgenstein, *Tractatus Logico-Philosophicus*, trans. C. K. Ogden (1921; repr., London: Routledge, 1990), para 6.53.
3. Wittgenstein, *Investigations*, para. 309.
4. Ibid., para. 558.
5. Ibid., para. 583.
6. Ibid., para. 511.
7. Peter Noever, "The Theme," in *The End of Architecture? Documents and Manifestos: Vienna Architecture Conference*, ed. Peter Noever (Munich: Prestel, 1993), 9.

of "neutral architecture as a neuter, as putty in the hands of developers," and warns that "architecture as a professional, lifeless product would be the holocaust of every spatial concept."[8] Eric Owen Moss asserts that, contrary to common belief, "architecture isn't art or shelter or progress or the form of cities," but rather "a fight against nihilism."[9] In his preface, Frank Gehry dismisses the whole discussion altogether: "Architecture, after all, is about building buildings.... I guess finally I am optimistic that all of you will get to work and will not have to sit around and worry about the end of architecture."[10]

Nonetheless, worry they did. Speakers addressed the question in idiosyncratic ways that reflected the uniqueness of their own practices. However, in their diverse contributions, they mostly understood "the end of architecture" in two main ways, similar to many other architects before them, as "terminus" or as "telos."

End used as the terminus of architecture evokes the idea of destruction or extinction, of a world where architecture no longer exists. "End *qua* termination" is one case of a word driving a line of thought, rather than a thought finding its home in a word. After all, what would the disappearance of architecture even imply? It provokes a productive thought experiment in which language acts like a spectrometer that shows indirect readings of an otherwise unthinkable notion: a world where the word *architecture* falls into disuse. The word *architecture* wouldn't be spoken in reference to a practice as we know it, nor to a historical activity that once existed, nor even to a memory. It wouldn't be spoken at all. The sense in which we use the word architecture today would not have migrated to another term, nor would traces of its practice linger in others. The prospect of "the end of architecture *qua* terminus" propels our imagination to apocalyptic scenarios of civilizational collapse. What cataclysm could cause such an event? What would a postarchitectural existence look like? What radical modifications to our mode of living would allow for it? We can almost hear Wittgenstein's voice here, striking the crux of the question: "Well, what do you mean by the word *architecture*?"

While "end as terminus" tends toward a doomsday sense, it's actually used more modestly. Far from doing away with architecture, it focuses instead on a certain way of conceiving, characterizing, or conducting architecture. It's "the end of architecture-*as-understood-in-a-certain-way*." Case in point, the text on the back cover of *The End of Architecture?* translates its original question into: "The end of

8. Coop Himmelblau, "The End of Architecture," in Noever, *The End of Architecture?*, 17.
9. Eric Owen Moss, "Out of Place Is the One Right Place," in Noever, *The End of Architecture?*, 61.
10. Frank O. Gehry, "Preface," in Noever, *The End of Architecture?*, 11, 13.

experimentation, of grand designs? What is the role of contemporary architecture in our increasingly complex society? What relation does it have to history, to tradition? What architectural programs or urban concepts can meet the demands of our age?"[11] The critiques implicit in these questions do not lead to the eradication of any form of practice or work that we might refer to as "architecture," as proved by how we continue to practice and speak of architecture in the 32 years since the book's publication, with no sign of stopping any time soon. What we mean when we use the word *architecture* may have changed, though, and this is what the speakers were getting at: the obsolescence of a particular idea of architecture.

End is also meant as the purpose or function of architecture. The notion harkens back to the Ancient Greek concept of *telos*, the finality toward which something happens, or the reason for which it exists, or the goal by which its being is fulfilled. Aristotle, in the *Nicomachean Ethics*, points to various examples of telos, namely "to health in the case of medicine, to victory in that of strategy, to a house in architecture, and to something else in each of the other arts; but in every pursuit or undertaking it describes the end [telos] of that pursuit or undertaking, since in all of them it is for the sake of that end that everything else is done."[12] These finalities are not at all the same for Aristotle. Some are ends toward other ends, and others are ends in themselves. For example, the purpose of the eye is to see, but sight itself has a higher purpose, such as for perceiving things or, higher still, for living well.

In the *Physics*, Aristotle notes how "the builder must know what the house is to be like and also that it is built of bricks and timber." He continues, "And further the same inquiry must embrace both the purpose or end and the means to that end [telos]. And the nature is the goal for the sake of which the rest exists."[13] The telos as purpose determines what something is, or its "nature," not only insofar as it justifies *why* something exists, but also *how*. Its purpose conditions its characteristics, shaped in order to perform its *why*. Thus, in a work of architecture, the function of a type of building determines certain spatial features or technical characteristics.

These two ways in which we speak of "the end of architecture" both point toward a matter of *defining* architecture: telos defines architecture in terms of its guiding purposes; termination tears down definitions of architecture. These senses are neither the same nor do they necessarily belong hand in hand. For example, the "end as telos"

11. Peter Noever, *The End of Architecture?*, back cover.
12. Aristotle, *Nichomachean Ethics*, trans. H. Rackham (Cambridge, MA: Harvard University Press), sec. I.vii.1.
13. Aristotle, *Physics, Volume 1: Books 1–4*, trans. P. H. Wicksteed and F. M. Cornford (Cambridge, MA: Harvard University Press), sec II.ii, 194a.

presupposes that a definition is teleological to some extent, while "end as terminus" excludes the evolution or deepening of certain meanings rather than their rejection for another. Aristotle exposes the dangers of conflating "telos" and "terminus" when using the word *end*, in a sidenote in the *Physics*: "(A confusion on this point betrayed the poet into the unintentionally comic phrase in reference to a man's death: 'He has reached the end, for the sake of which he was born.')"[14]

There is, however, a sense in which one follows from the other: the determination of a telos in one definition may imply the terminus of another. This point is taken up by Jacques Derrida, for whom language was of utmost importance, but whose embrace of wordplay and ambiguity in thought sets him apart from Wittgenstein. In his talk "The Ends of Man," delivered in 1968 at an anthropology conference, Derrida reflects on Heidegger's notion of "Being" in the following terms: "In the thought and the language of Being, the end of man has always been prescribed, and this prescription has never served except to modulate the equivocality of the *end*, in the interplay of *telos* and *death*."[15] Derrida exposes an inherent connection between thinking what it means to exist *qua* the central defining characteristic of humankind – what Heidegger defined as *Dasein* – and our finitude, or the prospect of death, as the condition, and even the motivation, from which that thinking takes place. In other words, our mortality defines us, not only as a necessary feature of our existence, but also by compelling and conditioning our questioning of our purpose. This interplay, contained in the linguistic ambiguity of the word *end*, is also reflected in our activities – such as architecture – and their *ends*.

Of course, unlike Wittgenstein, whose philosophical project consisted in outlining and remaining within the margins of what could be said, Derrida worked along the outer edges of those margins. The linguistic confusion that Wittgenstein saw as clouding thought was the tool Derrida used to pursue it. As he writes, "In the reading of this interplay, the following chain of events can be taken in all of its senses: the end of man is the thought of Being, man is the end of the thought of Being, the end of man is the end of the thought of Being. Man has always been his proper end; that is, the end of what is proper to him. The being has always been its proper end; that is, the end of what is proper to it."[16]

Philosophers have also disagreed about the ends of philosophy.

14. Ibid.
15. Jacques Derrida, "The Ends of Man," *Philosophy and Phenomenological Research* 30, no. 1 (September 1969): 55.
16. Ibid.
17. Ziva Frieman, ed., "Roundtable Discussion," in *The End of Architecture?*, 126.
18. Ludwig Wittgenstein, "The Blue Book," in *The Blue and Brown Books: Preliminary Studies for the "Philosophical Investigations"* (New York: Harper, 1965), 28.

Vienna Architecture Conference, The End of Architecture?, June 15, 1992, MAK–Austrian Museum of Applied Arts, Vienna. Spread from Peter Noever, ed., *The End of Architecture? Documents and Manifestos: Vienna Architecture Conference*, 1993.

3. The Ends of Definitions

As the Vienna Architecture Conference came to a close, Zaha Hadid let out a frustrated remark: "If we meet again, we have to make sure that the words we use mean the same to all of us."[17] Hadid's reaction to the idiosyncratic and often conflicting formulations of architecture's conditions, definitions, and vocabulary points to a linguistic difficulty. The issue doesn't lie in the shortcomings of language as such because it would be folly to think that if we were more meticulous and dug deeper into each word that we would find its unequivocal meaning. Even Wittgenstein, whose early work advocated for efforts toward discerning a direct correlation between logic and language, would later rectify his statements and concede that insofar as meaning in language is based on our use of it, then "ordinary language is all right."[18]

When the architects in Vienna presented their alternative accounts of architecture, they were not describing how the word *architecture* is commonly used or recognized. Instead, they were describing what they would like architecture to be, or how they would like it to work, and even what they wished the world were like in order for such an activity to exist. Describing the desired meaning of a word defines the desire, but not the word. Nor, as the speakers might wish, does it suffice to redefine it. The description of a word in different terms than those in which it is used is not a redefinition of the word but an erroneous definition.

This is not to say that the meanings of words don't change. However, meaning only changes when our use of a word changes. The definition of architecture could change if our practice of architecture changes. Similarly, describing things according to our wishes or expectations can have the power to change what we do to meet those wishes and expectations, but these descriptions will only constitute a definition once they match the way the word *architecture* is collectively used.

In the case of architecture, reigning and alternative definitions can be expressed discursively – as at the Vienna conference – but also, and primarily, through design – as in the work of several conference participants. Architectural practice participates in this process of redefining architecture, whether or not it is explicit, conscious, or even desired by the architects. After all, the act of designing presupposes an understanding of what architecture is or ought to be, from its irreducible telos to the means toward it. This conception may be blurry or transparent, total or fragmented, original or borrowed, but the work will always display and enforce it. With textual definition, every one of these built definitions contrasts with some other sense of what architecture is or ought to be. And if it seems like the words begin to lose their force and persuasiveness the deeper we probe into definitions of architecture, it's because architecture's activity surpasses what can be properly pinned down by language. Architecture touches the domain of what Wittgenstein thinks we cannot speak about, that which lies beyond language, and that which we would do best to simply "respond to . . . with a gesture"[19]

Whether through discourse or design, the act of defining architecture selects and coalesces pieces and impressions of meanings into a tangible form, rendering them graspable and operable. What the definition serves is then twofold. On the one hand, it materializes our understanding of what *architecture* means. On the other hand, it presents a clear target for critiques, as well as for aspirations of what architecture ought to be. In both cases, the definition functions as a reference point, either to rally around or to move away from. In no case does it pin down what architecture "actually" is in a determinate sense.

Architectural works constitute a historical record of changing meanings throughout time. On the other hand, they are not simply passive receptacles of their times. Like

19. Ludwig Wittgenstein, *Culture and Value* (Chicago: Chicago University Press, 2006), MS 156a 25r, 1932/1934.
20. Ludwig Wittgenstein, *Zettel* (Oxford: Blackwell, 1967), para. 447.

art, architecture consistently resists definitions. Respectively, architecture can reinforce dominant definitions or actively lead the charge against them. Revolutionary ruptures in its traditions come from regarding definitions as claims to disprove, constraints to break free from, targets to be shot down. At the same time, there is reassurance and solidity in working within certain set terms. The limits that outline a definition may thus be both that *within* which or that *around* which the architect works.

The recurrence of the question "the end of architecture?" isn't a sign of failure, as it might appear in a technoscientific view of progress, in which each development constitutes an improvement on the previous one. Nor is architecture's deliberate effort at compromising the limits of its definitions a self-defeating endeavor. Its irresolvable repetition does not make the question pointless either. Instead, it reflects our active engagement with a continuous process of redefining what we mean by architecture. This constant process of clarification is a necessary component of the discipline's self-renewal and, as such, a telos without terminus. As Wittgenstein said of philosophy, we can also say of architecture: "But in that case we never get to the end of our work! – Of course not, for it has no end."[20]

André Patrão is a senior researcher at ETH Zürich, in the Chair of the History of Art and Architecture. He is also a researcher at the EPFL, in the Lab of Architecture, Criticism, History, and Theory.

Observations on Logistics

The world has become a logistical landscape hidden from view. It is not the resources, goods, and products that humanity possesses and consumes that have brought the Anthropocene upon us, but rather the economy that enables this possession and consumption. Take Slovakian sod, for example. Known for its hydro-permeability, it is ideal for football fields and is thus used in stadiums all over Europe. Here, turf supplier Richter Rasen replaces the sod on the 86,400-square-foot playing field at Olympic Stadium, in the Berlin Olympic Park, home to Hertha BSC. The turf and any necessary working machines were loaded onto 30 trucks and transported over 400 miles from Slovakia to Berlin. Before returfing begins, approximately 550 tons of worn-out lawn are shipped off and recycled to serve as highway greenery or horticultural material. All of this happens twice a year. In these moments, the logistical landscape, which had been hiding in plain sight, becomes visible.

– Ludwig Engel

Zara Pfeifer, *Rollrasen*, 2022–2023
Published in *Space Issues*, Sandberg Instituut, 2023. Photo courtesy the photographer.

Justin Beal

Architecture at the End of the World

On an incandescent September afternoon last year, my nine-year-old daughter and I sat on a bench eating ice cream in the empty plaza of the Manhattan West development that links the Moynihan Train Hall to Hudson Yards. We had just walked the new spur of the High Line and were resting in the shade of a construction barrier, watching a janitor with a backpack vacuum suck up spotted lanternflies off the pavement at the base of an office tower. No one knows exactly why *Lycorma delicatula* are so attracted to tall buildings, but one popular theory is that they are lousy fliers – they can generate thrust but not much lift – so they are genetically programmed to find the tallest tree around and launch themselves into the wind. Incapable of distinguishing structure from flora, they climb buildings. They also seem to be particularly attracted to glass for reasons that may have to do with surface texture or temperature. Either way, they flock in hordes to one of the most unnatural structures we have ever created – the glass skyscraper. There were hundreds of lanternflies that afternoon, maybe thousands, rolling about on the pavement or climbing sluggishly skyward in search of a breeze on that windless day. A crowd of hapless newcomers wearing exquisite scarlet gowns beneath their blush polka-dot trench coats. They were delivered here by the movements of global capital only to be received with that most malignant vitriol reserved for unwelcome immigrants. Each one disappeared up the vacuum tube. *thwup. thwup. thwup.* "It feels unfair," my daughter offered, licking melting ice cream off her fingers. "Aren't we an invasive species too?"

* * *

The HBO series *The Last of Us* begins with a cold open of two epidemiologists being interviewed in 1968 by a talk show host. The subject is pandemics. When the host asks one of the doctors what his greatest pandemic fear is, he replies, stone-faced, that it is not a viral or bacterial pandemic but a mind-controlling fungal infection that poses the greatest existential threat to mankind.

In the ensuing monologue, the doctor describes a strain of pathogenic Cordyceps capable of infecting humans and controlling their minds and bodies "like a puppeteer with a marionette." The science is based on the Cordyceps fungus *Ophiocordyceps unilateralis*, which can enter the body of a carpenter ant, feed on its host from within, and multiply its own cells until it makes up nearly half of its host's body mass. Once established, the fungal cells push needlelike mycelia into the ant's muscles and send chemical signals to its brain, directing it to climb a tree and clamp its mandibles onto a vein on the underside of a leaf. The fungus emits sticky threads that lash the ant to the leaf, and then a stalk violently erupts from the host's head, showering spores onto the unsuspecting ants working on the forest floor below.

When his colleague challenges the notion that Cordyceps could survive in animals as warm-blooded as humans, the epidemiologist concedes that while that may be true for now, a small shift in global temperature might be enough for Cordyceps to adapt to higher temperatures. "One gene mutates," he speculates, and mankind could be reduced to a profusion of "puppets with poisoned minds permanently fixed on one unifying goal, to spread the infection to every last human alive."

The Last of Us is based on the hugely popular video game of the same name, created by Neil Druckmann's company Naughty Dog for Sony PlayStation in 2013. The HBO series was cowritten and codirected by Druckmann and Craig Mazin (best known for the 2019 ecocatastrophe drama *Chernobyl*) and is widely considered the best screen adaptation of a video game to date. Like the game, the series follows Joel (Pedro Pascal) as he escorts the teenage Ellie (Bella Ramsey), who, in a familiar trope of the zombie genre, is immune to the infection and may be humanity's last hope for salvation, across an America ravaged by a pathogenic Cordyceps fungus.

Pascal and Ramsey are excellent in the leading roles, but the astonishing intricacies of the series' overgrown, moldering cities are the show's greatest asset. Production designer John Paino, armed with a per-episode budget rumored to have exceeded that of most *Game of Thrones* installments, and relying far less on computer-generated imagery than one might expect, erected entire cities on location in Alberta, rendering the imagery of Druckmann's digital game world with meticulous, uncanny verisimilitude.

This is not a boilerplate dystopic wasteland, not the Malthusian grisaille of Cormac McCarthy's *The Road* (2006). Instead, it is a landscape of infrastructure repossessed – verdant urban canyons with buildings toppling like the trunks

Abandoned and flooded hotel lobby, a scene from the HBO series *The Last of Us*, 2023.

of ancient trees and nature repossessing abandoned architecture like coral making a reef in the carcass of a sunken ship. The world of *The Last of Us* is beautiful, teeming with wildlife and tangled foliage and, by any estimation, thriving. I was reminded at times of the moments of urban rewilding in Richard Matheson's *I am Legend* (1954), but the closest literary precedent might be Alan Weisman's 2007 bestseller *The World Without Us*.

Weisman's meticulous work of speculative science-*non*fiction opens with a simple question: If the human race vanished from the planet tomorrow, what would remain in a day, a year, a century? "How would nature respond," Weisman asks, "if it were suddenly relieved of the relentless pressures we heap on it?" *The World Without Us* is a methodical study of life after the Anthropocene. It was also a key reference for Druckmann, and the texture of his game world is clearly indebted to Weisman's vivid descriptions of life after *Us*.

Like all postapocalyptic stories, *The Last of Us* and *The World Without Us* play on how difficult it is for humans to imagine a world where we are not the dominant species. They both suggest that what we have truly endangered is not the planet but our ability to thrive on it. Even our most conscientious anxieties about "destroying the planet" are inherently self-centered because we tend to conflate the idea of an Earth uninhabitable by humans with an Earth incapable of sustaining life. We are damaging the ecosystem we inhabit, to be sure, but to say that we are destroying the planet is to grossly underestimate the planet's resiliency. The constant refrain that runs throughout *The World Without Us* is that in the face of an uncertain future, "the only real prediction you can make is that life will go on."

Some of the best television shows use genre as misdirection, and while *The Last of Us* leans on the conventions of the zombie apocalypse film, it is, at its emotional core, the story of an evolving relationship between a surrogate father and daughter, set within a parable of a ravaged ecosystem that is fighting back against a species that took it for granted. The entrancingly grotesque, often beautiful, saprophytic monsters in *The Last of Us* are not undead, they are not humans possessed by black magic or mad with infection, but rather mycelium in human form. Under the control of the Cordyceps, the mycologist Merlin Sheldrake observes in his 2020 book *Entangled Life: How Fungi Make Our Worlds, Change Our Minds & Shape Our Futures*, the carpenter ant loses any agency it might have had. "In physiological, behavioral, and evolutionary terms, the ant *becomes* a fungus." These are not zombies, this is nature exacting revenge, with an extraordinary, networked mycelial intelligence.

It is a fundamental tenet of the Anthropocene that our sense of superiority over nature is predicated on the illusion of our unparalleled intelligence. The horror of *The Last of Us* resides in the question of what it means, to borrow a phrase from urban historian Mike Davis's 1998 book Ecology of Fear, for us to "confront, for the first time, what it might be like to be on the receiving end of imperial conquest." And it is hard to imagine an adversary better suited to undo the damage we have left behind. There are fungi that can digest plastics and fungi that can break down oil. In her extraordinary 2015 study of matsutake foragers, *The Mushroom at the End of the World: On the Possibility of Life in Capitalist Ruins*, anthropologist Anna Lowenhaupt Tsing notes that after Hiroshima was devastated by an atomic bomb, "the first living thing to emerge from the blasted landscape was a matsutake mushroom."

* * *

In the spring of 2023, I was among a cohort of visiting critics at the final reviews of a first-year studio at the Yale School of Architecture. We had been invited to review the work of 60 architecture students over the course of six hours. At the conclusion of the reviews, we gathered for plastic cups of prosecco and an informal debriefing on the day's discussions. As the conversation drew to a close, an architect visiting from a prominent multinational firm called the group to attention and implored the students to "*never* stop thinking about the environment." A silence fell over the room as everyone nodded in righteous agreement. It struck me as an uncomfortable moment.

Ecology is currently the singular obsession of the profession, and thorny questions of how architects can lighten their impact on the environment are top of mind everywhere, from informal discussions among practitioners to the Venice Architecture Biennale. As the environmental impact of the global building industry becomes better understood, architects have found themselves in an uncomfortable position. Quantifying the environmental footprint of an entire industry is complicated, but it is now widely accepted that the built environment is accountable for about 40 percent of global greenhouse emissions. This is a huge number, surpassed only by that of the oil and gas industries, and simply put, there is no way to combat climate change without a radical reduction of energy consumption in this sector.

Considering those statistics, admonishing architecture students about climate change can begin to feel a bit like lecturing to a group of lumberjacks about the virtues of forest conservation. They can fill their models and renderings with green roofs and solar panels, cork walls and thermal barriers, but the brutal reality is that it is nearly impossible to build a new building without incurring a degree of negative ecological impact. For some, this reality can have a paralyzing effect. A colleague of mine recently bemoaned the difficulty of teaching basic design principles to students who find themselves wrestling with the existential question of how to make architecture if all architecture is "bad."

Architects, by nature, like to solve problems. The sort of people who gravitate toward the profession tend to be idealistic, so feelings of complicity can weigh heavily on their conscience. Unfortunately for them, architecture is also an artform uniquely beholden to the whims of developers and financiers. Building requires capital, and capital demands growth, and growth tends to be difficult to achieve without ecological impact on a planet with finite natural resources.

For most of the early 21st century, conservation efforts in the building industry have been focused on "in-use" energy – the energy used to heat or to cool, to keep the lights on, and to manage water and waste. This allowed designers and developers to present new buildings as "green" through certification programs like LEED. As our understanding of resource consumption has become more sophisticated, attention has turned to the sum of all the energy required to extract, produce, transport, and assemble the materials used in construction. Upward of 85 percent of a building's carbon footprint comes from this "embodied" energy. If the cement industry were a country, for example, it would be the third largest emitter of carbon dioxide in the world, after China and the US.

At Hudson Yards, steps from the bench where my daughter and I watched the disoriented lanternflies languish in the heat, the relatively inconsequential gestures touted by the project's developer – including stormwater recycling and pollinator gardens – do little to justify the colossal amount of energy embedded in the acres of new office space foisted upon a city that simply does not need them. In *Log* 47 (Fall 2019), Elisa Iturbe dubbed projects like these, where capitalist logic wins out over ecological reasoning and common sense, "carbon forms." Drawing attention away from their ecological impact by focusing on technologies that increase efficiency, these projects "dislocate the origin of the climate crisis from the dominant political, economic, and spatial organizations that are its cause," Iturbe writes. Architecture, she warns, cannot begin to address the causes of the climate crisis without first recognizing the extent to which contemporary architecture and urbanism is subsumed by the logic of the fossil economy and the carbon-fueled myth of unlimited growth.

* * *

In January 2021, Saudi Crown Prince, and de facto ruler, Mohammed bin Salman appeared on state television to announce plans for a new linear city in the northeast corner of the Arabian Desert. The city, to be known as the Line, will run straight through more than a hundred miles of desert, from the outskirts of Tabuk to the Red Sea. It will be 1,650 feet tall, 650 feet wide, mirrored on the exterior and home to nine million people. The scale is difficult to comprehend, though it might help to imagine an inhabited wall, as thick as two football fields and taller than the original World Trade Center towers, running, uninterrupted, from New York through Philadelphia, to Wilmington, Delaware.

The Line is part of Neom, one of 14 petrodollar-fueled "giga projects" conceived by bin Salman to help propel Saudi Arabia into a less oil-dependent future. It may be the most audacious carbon form ever conceived. Billed as a carless and carbonless vertical city – powered entirely by renewable energy, watered entirely by desalination plants, and connected by a hyperloop – the Line comes with extravagant but absurd promises about sustainability, reliant, in many cases, on technology that does not yet exist (there has also been talk of a giant artificial moon, flying taxis, robot maids, and a beach with glow-in-the-dark sand). Even with these fantasy technologies, the claims of sustainability seem to ignore the prodigious amount of steel, concrete, water, and energy required to colonize one of the least hospitable environments on Earth. And the obvious, if unprecedented, impact that a 100-mile long, skyscraper-height, mirrored wall would have on wildlife mocks official claims that the Line is "designed to protect and enhance nature." On the inside, renderings show a world of glass walls faceted like towering expanses of synthetic basalt, with lush, terraced forests and waterfalls cascading down over dramatically cantilevered living spaces.

Even if the hyperloop works and climate control keeps the chasm between the city's two towering walls temperate, it is still unclear why exactly anyone would want to live in the Line. Developers boast of a "smart-city" powered by artificial intelligence that will monitor citizens and use predictive software and data models to find ways to improve daily life (with residents being paid for submitting data). This amount of surveillance would be a dicey proposition under any circumstance, but in a country where decades-long prison sentences are handed down for mild criticism of the regime, it seems something close to self-incarceration. It is difficult to imagine, after all, a more authoritarian architectural typology than the wall.

In light of all these ethical and environmental concerns, what is most surprising about Neom is not its ambition but the number of designers who were willing to sign on. The list has included some of the biggest names in the field – Bjarke Ingels Group, Heatherwick Studio, HOK, Coop Himmelblau, and Pritzker Prize laureates Zaha Hadid Architects and Morphosis, whose principal Thom Mayne was the Line's master planner. Sir Norman Foster stepped down from Neom's advisory board after the brutal murder and dismemberment of Jamal Khashoggi in 2018, but Foster + Partners continues to work on multiple Saudi airports that will serve the area. Rem Koolhaas's OMA drew up a scheme for a section of the Line but appears to no longer be involved. Neom officially cut ties with Adjaye Associates after allegations of sexual improprieties were raised against David Adjaye in 2023, suggesting that even a regime with an egregious record of human rights violations is not above passing moral judgment.

It is easy enough to condemn architects for engaging with such a morally suspect enterprise, but architecture is a tough business, and commissions of this magnitude come perhaps once in a generation. There are rumors that the lucrative consulting contracts for Neom are helping to keep a number of design offices in London afloat in an uncertain economy, but there is no way to verify this because Neom management requires all architects to sign restrictive nondisclosure agreements.

The involvement of one architect in particular feels especially complicated, and a bit sad. As part of the Archigram group in the 1960s, Peter Cook designed the pop megalopolis Plug-in City – a high-tech, high-rise megastructure comprised of capsule components that could plug in to an enormous infrastructural scaffold. Cook was a provocateur, but unlike many of his peers in the counterculture, he always maintained that Archigram was apolitical. At the age of 87, Cook now finds himself working on a project that looks, superficially at least, astonishingly similar to his own visions from long ago, but it may be harder for him to disavow politics now than it was in the 1960s.

In many ways, the Line is a pastiche of past avant-gardes – in addition to Archigram, there are echoes of linear cities proposed by Arturo Soria y Mata in the 1880s and Edward Chambless in 1910; Le Corbusier's 1932 plan for Algiers or Kenzō Tange's 1960 plan of Tokyo Bay; Yona Friedman's 1958 Spatial City or Constant's New Babylon, 1959–74 – but the most obvious inspiration is a project imagined by the Italian neo-Marxist radical architecture collective Superstudio, in 1969. The Continuous Monument, presented in a series of seductive, nihilistic collages, was a mirrored megalith, an inexorable and unescapable belt of Cartesian development plowing across oceans and deserts and engulfing Manhattan. The Continuous Monument was conceived as a "negative utopia," a provocation and a satire, a riposte to the technological idealism of modernism and a critique of the hubris of capitalism and the relentless urbanization of the planet. Superstudio cofounder Adolfo Natalini called it a warning against "the horrors architecture had in store," yet it seems to have been embraced, without irony, by Mayne and bin Salman as a viable model for the city of the future.

If architecture is an interest of bin Salman's, video games are an obsession, and the logic of a gamer's imagination is as present in the design of the Line as the palimpsest of the modernist avant-garde. The hundred-mile cavern city of hanging gardens and translucent bridges is organized according to a principle touted by the Neom team as "zero-gravity urbanism." It is a hard term to parse, but it more easily evokes the dystopian intricacies of a video game world than any realistic plan for a city beholden to, well, gravity. Ridley Scott's 1982 film *Blade Runner*, an adaptation of Philip K Dick's 1968 book *Do Androids Dream of Electric Sheep*, comes immediately to mind, which is unsurprising given that bin Salman reportedly directed designers of the project toward an aesthetic of cyberpunk – a term fittingly defined by the author Bruce Sterling, in the preface to a 2003 edition of William Gibson's *Burning Chrome* (1982), as a "combination of lowlife and high tech."

In addition to architects and urban planners, bin Salman has enlisted an army of Hollywood special effects consultants – including Olivier Pron, concept artist of *Snowpiercer* (2013); Nathan Crowley, production designer of *Interstellar* (2014); and Jeff Julian, art director of the film adaptation of *I Am Legend* (2007) and *World War Z* (2013) – to bring his vision to life. It is here where the parallel narratives of *The Last of Us* and the Line begin to converge. The Line comes from the same lineage as *The Last of Us*, from the fractured dystopias of video games and zombie films, but it emerges without a conscience. The crown prince seems to have internalized cyberpunk aesthetics, perhaps even the aesthetic of the architectural avant-garde, without understanding what any of it means.

I have been tempted to go see the Line for myself, but for now there is nothing more than a few excavators pawing at the surface of a vast desert. In April 2024, Bloomberg reported that plans for the Line were being scaled back dramatically, with only one and a half miles of construction forecast to be completed by 2030. HOK and Coop Himmelblau are no longer associated with the project, and in July, Thom Mayne abruptly stepped down from his role as master planner. Some minor Neom attractions are coming along, but it is my strong suspicion that the main event will never evolve beyond the renderings. The Line does not need to exist to achieve its objective. It is an architectural spectacle for social media and a marketing pitch to sell a story of progress and reform to foreign investors – a bit of soft power to launder the reputation of a regime built on a particularly brutal form of hard power.

* * *

In 2016, the hotelier Ernesto Coppel Kelly invited architect Tatiana Bilbao to work on a major park project in the coastal resort city of Mazatlán, Mexico. The brief was to reclaim and restore a 74-acre green space, which included a small lagoon, so that it could both support natural life and help to manage water flow during periods of heavy rainfall and flooding. Bilbao reintroduced resilient endemic vegetation to the lagoon and designed a network of raised pathways to allow pedestrian access without disrupting the ecosystem. It was a simple and sensitive solution.

As work on the project progressed, Bilbao was offered a second commission to design an aquarium planned for the south end of the park. She was hesitant at first. Bilbao, who runs a medium-sized Mexico City office, is particularly sensitive to the myopia of human-centered design. She knew from the outset that designing an aquarium would mean working against the conventions of an architectural typology predicated on the fantasy of human control over nature. She accepted the commission on the condition that the aquarium's purview would be limited to exploring and protecting the extraordinary biodiversity in the Sea of Cortez, one of the richest ecosystems in the world. This meant, among other things, no penguins.

Bilbao approached the commission with a strategy of futurist storytelling. She began by speculating that sometime around the year 2100, the city of Mazatlán was inundated by a rising Pacific. The floodwaters receded by 2227, and when humans returned to the area in 2289, they discovered a massive ruin now teeming with marine life left behind by the retreating ocean. They had no idea when or why this building had been constructed, but they embraced it with the understanding that, we, as human beings, are just another part of the natural world. The task of the architect, then, was only to open pathways, create staircases, and unlock the possibilities of this found structure animated by a century of aquatic life. It was from this point of departure that she began designing the building that now houses the Sea of Cortez Research Center.

On Earth Day last year, both Bilbao and Paino were among the speakers in The World Around Contemporary Architecture Summit at the Guggenheim Museum in New York. As I sat in the basement auditorium listening to Paino describe how he transformed Canadian backlots into the overgrown ruins of American cities, my mind wandered back to the third chapter of *The World Without Us*, which includes a description of the unravelling of the Metropolitan Museum in the years after human extinction. I considered a similar situation unfolding above my head at the Guggenheim. I began

Tatiana Bilbao Estudio, Sea of Cortez Research Center, Mazatlan, Sinaloa, Mexico, 2023. Photo: Iwan Baan.

to imagine what Frank Lloyd Wright's museum might look like after its skylight gives way and seeds blow in from the park – small dogwoods and oaks, butterfly weeds and skunk cabbages reclaiming the spiral rotunda. Rainwater trickles down the rotunda's ramp turning it into a mountain stream. Without climate control, mold and fungi make quick work of the paintings, but the bronzes, covered in moss, might remain unscathed until the entire building gives way beneath them (bronze, Weisman observes, is one of the most resilient materials humans have ever created).

Paino, joined on stage by filmmaker and architect Liam Young and curator Lucia Pietroiusti, discussed the painstaking work of constructing a digital game world as a set for human actors. Paino approached world-building much as a game designer might, striving to create a total environment for actors to explore in depth rather than limiting his scope to the precise set pieces required for the shots needed to move the plot forward. The result gives the environment in which the show unfolds, particularly in the dense urban areas, an uncanny realism. In the show's second episode, Joel and Ellie find themselves in an expansive, flooded hotel lobby, in Boston. Three ducks swim in the muddy water, a frog hops noisily along the keyboard of an abandoned piano, and a waterfall cascades down from a balcony above. The scene's action unfolds gradually as the camera's gaze wanders inquisitively through the space.

The ray exhibition tank in the coastal area of the Sea of Cortez Research Center, Mazatlan, Sinaloa, Mexico, 2023. Photo: Iwan Baan.

With the image of a storyboard for the inundated lobby on the screen behind them, the conversation turned to the Anthropocene. For a long time, Young observed, human-centered design "has just been an alibi for engineering the world around our own needs and desires." Paino recalled asking himself, as he struggled to imagine a nearly post-human world, if the supremacy of the Cordyceps in *The Last of Us* was simply a natural part of evolution. He seemed to take this proposition very seriously. I was struck by how he described the landscapes his crew had created as spaces of hope rather than desolation – as evidence of nature restoring balance.

In a deft bit of curatorial orchestration by the event's organizer, Beatrice Galilee, Paino was followed after a break by Bilbao. As she ran through images of conceptual collages and working models of the Sea of Cortez Research Center (Bilbao prefers to develop designs by hand, rather than through digital media), it was impossible not to marvel at their resonance with the rewilded mise-en-scène of *The Last of Us*.

As she progressed to images of the building under construction in Mazatlán, it seemed to already be in a state of ruination, with ceilings open to the elements, vines creeping up concrete walls, and tidepools forming in open volumes on the roof. A pair of open-air staircases guide visitors up to the building's top floor, from which they descend into the aquarium via a central spiral stair. Nearby, vegetation cascades through another circular opening into a cenote-like courtyard below. Here, the building bears an uncanny resemblance to Lina Bo Bardi's Casa Coati in Salvador, Brazil, another intervention among ruins, and it possesses much of the same radical optimism that was so important to Bo Bardi's work.

Carson Chan, curator of the 2023 exhibition "Emerging Ecologies," at the Museum of Modern Art in New York, has described aquariums as "microcosms of how humanity endeavors to control the planet's ecosystem." The Sea of Cortez Research Center is not a perfect solution to the problems posed by the type. Its tanks still hold fish captive for human entertainment and its concrete walls still required massive amounts of embodied energy, but on the whole, the center creates a narrative that pushes back against the expectations of a carbon form by taking full advantage of the most powerful tool architects have at their disposal – storytelling. By changing the timeline, by moving beyond and back into the Anthropocene, Bilbao offers a glimpse into a world without people (without us) as a first step toward a less anthropocentric architecture.

In February 2024, I returned to Yale to listen to Bilbao give a lecture. When I arrived, the school's auditorium was at capacity, and students were lined up to get into an adjacent room with a live video feed. The overflow space was nearly at capacity as well, and a handful of administrators huddled nervously, considering options. They managed to get everyone in, but it was clear that something in Bilbao's approach to world-building was resonating with students.

At dinner after the lecture, I asked Bilbao if she had watched *The Last of Us* before the event at the Guggenheim. "Of course," she said. When I asked her how she felt about presenting after Paino, she said she was terrified. In the break between their presentations, Bilbao and Paino had crossed paths backstage and she urged him to stay long enough to see her talk because she thought it might interest him. When she was done, Paino approached Bilbao to say it was an amazing project and that he hoped someday she might find a way to get it built. To which she responded, "Those weren't renderings, John. My building is already there."

Justin Beal is an artist and writer based in New York. His first book *Sandfuture* was published by the MIT Press, in September 2021, and his writing has recently appeared in *Frieze*, *Harper's*, and *The Architect's Newspaper*. Beal teaches at Hunter College.

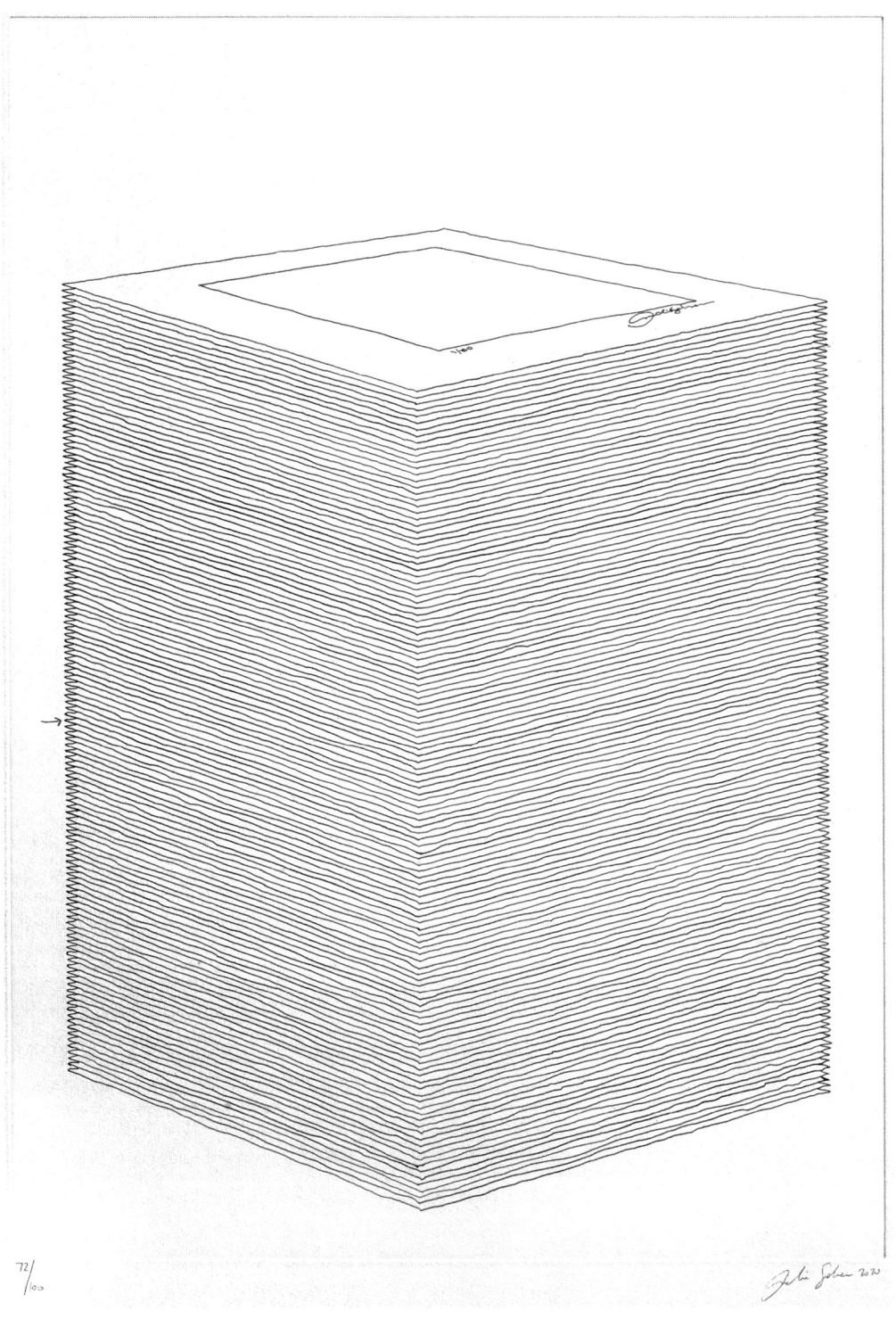

Analia Saban, *This One (Edition of 100)*, 2020. Etching with pencil, 36 7/8 by 28 1/4 inches. © 2020 Analia Saban and Gemini G.E.L. LLC.